Endorsements

"Augustine provides a comprehensive outline of the steps to follow, resources to utilize, and fundamentals of finding your next career."
MARY OLSON – Director of Recruitment, Chicago Tribune

"If you read one book in your career search, let Augustine's "Knocking" be it"
DIPAK JAIN – Dean, Kellogg School of Management, Northwestern University

"An unbelievably useful job handbook! This book covers the entire job search process, from beginning your job search to succeeding in your new job. One of the most thorough, yet concise, job search resources I have ever read."
HAL BECKER – Best Selling author of *Can I Have Five Minutes of Your Time?*

"Augustine's book is a fantastic resource that you should use and apply to land the job you want. As a former recruiter, he provides an excellent insiders perspective of what it takes to sell yourself in a tough job market."
DAVID SZARY – CEO and Founder, Recruiter Academy

"This book will completely prepare you for any professional interview – from your initial HR contact to your interview with an executive. It provides a roadmap for any candidate seeking to get ahead in the job market."
JOHN T. JIMENEZ – Chief Financial Officer, Air BP North America, Division of BP

"In an era where entry and mid-level jobs are migrating to developing markets such as China and India, it has become even more critical to prepare yourself, so as to differentiate yourself from the pack. This book provides immediate pay-back and should become that dog-eared book that you continually lend to your network of friends and colleagues."
JOHN QUINN – Senior Partner, DiamondCluster International

"The most important attribute of a company's growth is the caliber of people it hires. Augustine's book teaches you how to be that high caliber candidate that companies need. From preparing your resume to succeeding months after your first day on the job, *How Hard Are You Knocking* simply describes your path to success – every step of the way."
ERIC FLAMHOLTZ – Best-selling author of *Growing Pains,* CEO ManagementSystems Inc.

"This book is an excellent resource for international job seekers looking to understand the job search process and identify effective resources that will uncover job opportunities. Augustine's book is straightforward and easy to use. A must read for any international job seeker entering this job market.
RAMIRO DE FRANCISCO – Director, Export Operations, Quaker Oats, Division of PepsiCo International

"'*How Hard Are You Knocking?*' puts the power of finding a job where it belongs—in your hands. Explore the companies you admire. Understand what impresses hiring managers—and what doesn't. Learn to network, take control and get the job you want. Whether you're fresh out of school or back in the job market after a long absence, you'll find author Tim Augustine's down-to-earth approach refreshing and reassuring."
REBECCA KUCHAR – Vice President of Sales & Client Relationship Management, Pyramid Digital Solutions

How Hard
Are You Knocking?

How Hard Are You Knocking?

The Job Seekers' Guide to
Opening Career Doors

Timothy J. Augustine
with Rana Curcio

With a Foreword by

John A. Challenger,
CEO, Challenger, Gray and Christmas

Oakhill Press
Winchester, VA

10   9   8   7   6   5   4   3   2   1

Library of Congress Cataloging-in-Publication Data

Augustine, Timothy, 1971–
  How hard are you knocking? : the job seekers' guide to opening career doors /
Timothy J. Augustine ; with Rana Curcio ; with a foreword by John A. Challenger.
    p. cm.
  ISBN 1-886939-64-0 (pbk. : alk. paper)
  1. Job hunting. 2. Applications for positions. 3. Résumés (Employment)
4. Employment interviewing. I. Curcio, Rana, 1971– II. Title.

HF5382.7.A86 2004
650.14–dc22

2004056088

Oakhill Press
1647 Cedar Grove Road
Winchester, VA 22603
800-32-books
Printed in the United States of America

Contents

Foreword

Globalization, outsourcing, and corporate downsizing are a few of the significant challenges facing today's job market. These issues are forcing many people to look for new jobs, dust off their résumés, and develop creative strategies to differentiate their skills and abilities in a competitive job market. While the job market continues to adjust to economic challenges, job seekers need to uncover job opportunities and implement the strategies necessary to land a new job. Whether you are a college student preparing for your first job search or an experienced professional looking for a change, everyone is asking the same question: "How can I jump into the job market and learn to sell myself?"

Consider the case of Kathy, who was a senior at Northwestern University and preparing for her first professional job search. She had a few jobs during college as well as an internship in her field, and she really wanted to begin her career with an advertising agency. She began by researching potential firms, leveraging her network of contacts, and developing a strong résumé and cover letter. She was very successful in scheduling interviews and meeting with some of the largest firms in the city. However, she never received any job offers.

This type of situation can be frustrating for job seekers. In this case, Kathy's job search strategies were very good, including her preparation and the development of her résumé and cover letter. However, she did not spend enough time preparing for the interviews; as a result, she never quite knew how to respond to the questions. As you enter the job market, you need to consider what types of interviews you might encounter, the topics and questions that you'll be asked to address, and details associated with selling your skills and abilities. *How Hard Are You Knocking?* does a great job of preparing you for the interview. Augustine covers the types of interviews you will encounter, provides an excellent example of interview questions, and offers advice on salary negotiation and follow-up.

John, a seasoned software development manager, was forced to begin his job search after his position of fifteen years was eliminated. He walked into my office and simply said, "I was not prepared for this. I have not developed a résumé in ten years, nor have I interviewed since I joined my company. Unfortunately, I did not spend enough time building my professional network to tap into. Can you help me?" This situation often happens to professionals who have dedicated their life to their work.

The fears and questions of most job seekers begin with the daunting question of where and how to start their job search. Today's job market can be challenging, and job seekers who follow a well-developed plan and use specific tools can often differentiate themselves in the job market.

As America's foremost authority on helping people find new jobs, Challenger, Gray and Christmas has—throughout a forty-year history—helped thousands of job seekers find new jobs by providing them with best-practices job search support and training methods that we have developed through our research and experience. At Challenger, Gray and Christmas, we advise our clients on the following simple yet effective steps.

Step 1: Assess your abilities, experiences, and accomplishments.

This step helps increase your confidence and provides a solid foundation to help you develop a marketing message that you can highlight along with your abilities during the interview.

Step 2: Develop your marketing message.

Companies want to understand what you can do for them. Your marketing message needs to be concise while illustrating the value you bring. These factors should be highlighted in your results-oriented résumé.

Step 3: Use your network.

Build a strategy that leverages your personal network of family, friends, colleagues, and alumni. This resource could be the most important one you use during your job search. *How Hard Are You Knocking?* does a masterful job of helping you build and leverage your network.

Step 4: Target specific companies.

Use this book to help identify your target companies. Research those companies to find the opportunities that match your expectations.

Using a similar best-practices approach, Tim Augustine's *How Hard Are You Knocking?* offers smart career advice in an entertaining and easy-to-read format. Designed with today's pragmatic job seeker in mind, this concise career guide details the job search process in a "soup to nuts" fashion and in a straightforward manner. Whether you are a recent college graduate or a seasoned professional who just wants a refresher, this energetic book can provide you with the knowledge and skills necessary to obtain the ideal job.

Augustine not only covers the basics of résumé writing and interviewing, but also outlines how to assess your career goals, how to identify potential employers that match your career goals, how to effectively use your network to find a job, and how to develop a mutually beneficial relationship with recruiting and consulting firms. The detailed samples and anecdotes in *How Hard Are You Knocking?* breathe life into his clever suggestions and provide concrete examples for the reader. Augustine combines his professional experience in the field of human resources and expertise in hiring and recruiting with his global marketing experience to provide valuable tips for job seekers to effectively position and market their skills in order to set themselves apart from other prospective job applicants.

Good luck in your search.

JOHN A. CHALLENGER
Chief Executive Officer
Challenger, Gray and Christmas Inc.

Introduction

Why Should You Read This Book?

In this economy, many people are facing a tough job market. This book is designed for new job seekers or those who have been working for a while and are looking to find a new job, or even for those who are potentially making a career change. Frankly, you can't afford not to read and apply the job search techniques illustrated in this book! This book is essential to helping you build a solid job strategy as well as helping you fully understand all aspects of the job search process. You have either purchased this book because you are thinking of conducting a job search or you are already in the midst of one. Whatever the reason, you should find this book very useful in finding a new job. It is designed to be a short, concise resource guide that you can use to effectively build a job search strategy, find and utilize job search resources, develop a powerful résumé, prepare for the interview, and negotiate a starting salary.

The premise of the book is very simple. I wanted to develop a resource guide that was based on real examples and to provide the information in a format that was easy to read and understand. You should be able to read this book in a few hours and significantly increase your chances of job search success.

This book can be an invaluable resource to anyone looking for a new job. *How Hard Are You Knocking?* is a how-to career guide that illustrates proven best practices used to find a new job. Use this book as your guide to efficiently and dramatically improve your job search results.

Before you begin reading further, I would like to outline the job search process and provide an overview of this book.

The first step to an effective job search is the initial preparation. In this book, you work with a detailed outline that highlights the process you should follow to conduct a personal

Internal and External Assessment. This assessment process should flesh out your personal and professional goals as well as help you identify ideal criteria that your target companies should possess. The objective of the first chapter is to conduct this Internal and External Assessment, identify target company criteria, build a job search strategy, and identify fifteen target companies on which to focus your efforts.

The second step of an effective search is to conduct thorough research. I have identified and illustrated in the "Resources to Utilize" chapter various resources for you to use in researching companies, building your network, and uncovering open positions that match your career aspirations.

Once you conduct your assessments, build your job search strategy, and research your target companies, you need to prepare to make contact with your target companies. This contact includes your résumé and cover letter, your business attire (which can make a positive first impression), and the various interviews you conduct before you find the job you desire. This book provides you with effective techniques that can help you build a powerful résumé and marketing plan. In addition, the "Dressing the Part" chapter highlights professional attire etiquette by providing general guidelines as well as gender-based do's and don'ts. "The Spotlight: The Interview" chapter describes the types of interviews you might face, the interview topics that might be addressed, and the expectations following your first interview. This chapter helps you prepare for the series of interviews as well as providing methods to deal with salary negotiations and acceptance as well as rejection.

The final chapter covers your career development plan after you get your job. Based on my experience as a vice president of human resources I have found that the important time to make a positive first impression is within the first ninety days. Therefore, I present an extensive orientation program for you to follow that focuses on organizational areas you need to understand fully in order to become integrated with the company. This chapter is an important aspect of your job search and should be viewed as critical to your career success.

How Hard Are You Knocking? offers a broad view of the job search process and is designed to provide an effective set of guidelines for getting you started. Make sure you focus your energies on differentiating yourself from other job seekers. The proven techniques listed in this book have been studied and presented with fantastic success to thousands of job seekers.

Remember, the job market is filled with people looking for an open position. By reading this book, you can identify target companies and position yourself as the best person for a company, whether they have an opening or not. The most important guideline that you can follow is to maintain a positive attitude and remain motivated. If you use this book and apply these techniques to your search, your chances of success increase exponentially. I wish you the best of luck and hope you enjoy reading *How Hard Are You Knocking?*

Acknowledgments

Special thanks for the contributions from Gary Wilberg, Co-Owner and Managing Partner for the Herman Draack Company, an international human resource consulting firm specializing in executive recruitment, project outsourcing and human resource strategy implementation in Chicago, San Francisco and Washington D.C. Throughout his career, Gary has specialized in the field of contingent and retained recruiting and has helped national outplacement firms develop their clients' job search strategies.

Thanks also to the following people for their help and support for this book: Adele Revella, Hal Becker, Dana Curcio, Ramiro DeFrancisco, Eric Flamholtz, Ed Helvey, Kathy Jahnke, Dipak Jain, John Jimenez, Andy Kindler, Rebecca Kuchar, Eileen O'Connor, Mary Olson, Doug Pifer, John Quinn, David Szary, and Rodney Williams.

Finally, we would like to thank our families and friends for your love and continued support.

Chapter 1

Beginning Your Job Search

"Genius is 1 percent inspiration and 99 percent perspiration."
Thomas Edison

An actual job search can be time-consuming and frustrating. However, you can take steps to ensure that you spend your time wisely and efficiently. This chapter is designed to help you think about your strategy and target where to focus your energies. The rest of the book provides specific techniques and methods you can use to research companies, develop your résumé, prepare for the interview, and negotiate your starting salary.

The first step of the job search is to conduct a personal assessment, both internal and external. The following outline can be used as a guide for this assessment. Use it to document your goals, identify your career target, and develop steps to help you reach those goals. I have provided an example of an actual job search strategy in Figure 1 (see page 15). You should review this example after you have read through the Internal and External Assessments. Take out a sheet of paper and write down your answers to each of the questions. This activity serves two purposes. First, it forces you to think more carefully about your goals as you convert your desires into words. Second, it provides a constant reminder and reference as you move forward in your job search process. Look back at this list in later years and amend it as your career and life goals change.

The first assessment you need to complete is an Internal Assessment. This Internal Assessment is designed to uncover your own internal drivers. By identifying your internal drivers, you will be able to assess different positions and companies and establish your career direction. Ask yourself these questions and write down your answers. Feel free to list several answers to each question in bullet-point form. The idea is to get the thoughts down on paper and out of your mind. Honesty is important here. If, for example, you want to be close to your family most of the time, don't write down that you want a job that includes 75 percent travel.

This Internal Assessment can be a vital aspect of a successful job search. Based on my experience, the number-one reason that a new employee leaves a firm within six months is cultural misalignment. If you follow this Internal Assessment, you should be able to identify the types of companies where you can thrive. In one case, my firm had hired a sales manager with a great deal of experience. Prior to joining our small firm, he worked with three large multinational companies, where he was very successful. After a series of interviews, we selected him as our top candidate and offered him the job. Within the first month, we began to see a problem. Our culture was team-oriented and collaborative. This individual was highly competitive and seemed to take offense at sharing customer information. Within three months, we knew that we had made a mistake and had to terminate the relationship. Although he did not succeed at my firm, he was still a successful sales manager and thrived in large competitive environments. After conducting his exit interview, I found that he did not do an Internal Assessment and accepted the first offer he received, which was from my firm. Based on my experience, I highly recommend thinking through the Internal Assessment prior to starting your job search.

Internal Assessment

Define your personal and professional goals:

1. What are your strengths?

You should start your Internal Assessment by considering all of the attributes that you feel would be important to a potential employer. As you analyze your strengths, make sure you consider those strengths that set you apart from others. In addition, you need to be able to describe and illustrate your strengths to an interviewer.

_____

_____

_____

_____

_____

2. What type of culture would you thrive in?

Culture can be defined as the values, ideas, customs, skills, and interests of a people or group that are transferred, communicated, or passed along through the traditions and norms of an organization. As you consider culture, you need to truly understand an organization's values, which serve as a set of beliefs that drive the organization. Because organizational culture is often hard to define, you should consider what values are most important to you. For instance, are you interested in working for a company that believes that people are the most important asset of an organization or a company that values the customer as the most important asset? In addition, you might consider the following examples, which should help you further explore the type of culture that interests you most.

Autonomy vs. independence

Do you value a structured environment, or do you feel that too much structure is restrictive and intrusive? Do you prefer to work in a group or team to accomplish a task, or do you prefer individual tasks and projects?

Work-life balance

Are you interested in finding an organization that focuses its efforts on establishing a healthy work-life balance? Are you interested in a flexible culture that focuses on intrinsic rewards as a method of motivating its employees?

_____

_____

_____

_____

_____

_____

3. Where do you want to live now and in the future?

As part of an Internal Assessment, you need to consider all aspects of your life, including geographic location. Do you want to remain close to family and current friends? Are you interested in international assignments as part of your work? Are you interested in living near a large city? You must consider these and many other questions. This list can help you start.

_____

_____

4. What type of company would you like to work for?

Are you interested in working for a private or public organization? Are you interested in a specific industry, such as technology, financial services, insurance, or manufacturing? Are you interested in working for an international organization? Are you interested in finding an organization that has been selected as a "Best Place to Work" by national publications?

_____

_____

_____

_____

_____

5. What types of positions are you interested in?

As you consider potential positions, look beyond just the title. You should consider all aspects of a position, such as the skills, knowledge, experience, and education required. In addition, you should consider the following categories, which should help further define your ideal role:

Technical skills vs. functional skills

Are you interested in technical positions or functional positions? Technical positions typically have a specific area of expertise and develop their role around the specific knowledge or content of the work performed. Functional positions are typically more general in focus and include a broad range of tasks. A functional position, such as an accounting specialist, can provide a very transferable set of skills that apply to multiple positions, whereas a tax accountant focuses on specific skills highlighting your expertise.

Security and stability

Are you interested in a position that maintains a predictable workload? Are you interested in a specific position because of its stable role within the organization, such as an accountant's, versus a salesperson who relies on commissions?

Entrepreneurial inspiration

Are you interested in a position that provides the skills and knowledge that could help you develop your own business? Are you looking for a position that cultivates your creative imagination and allows you to develop new products or services? Are you looking for a position that provides creative challenges every day?

_____

_____

_____

_____

_____

6. What type of manager/boss motivates you?

Are you motivated by a manager who continually provides feedback or a boss who sets the direction and has a hands-off style? Are you motivated by a manager who leads by example and provides a lot of coaching? Are you interested in a manager who has connections and history with the organization?

_____

_____

_____

_____

7. Are you planning to continue your professional education?

Are you planning on professional development through education? If so, you should consider all goals that you would like to achieve, such as CPA, PHR, or CMM certifications, or formal educational milestones such as an MBA or another type of master's degree. In addition, you should consider those organizations that support continuing education and have a training or tuition reimbursement program.

_____

_____

_____

_____

8. What are your long-term goals?

Where do you want to be in five or ten years? For example: "I want to be a partner in an auditing firm." "I want to be vice president of sales for an international software company." "I want to be chief financial officer for a manufacturing organization." "I want to work in a marketing organization where I can cross-train and learn from others." Whatever your long-term goals, you need to continually measure specific steps that help you get there.

As you assess your career goals and target specific positions, you should also consider the types of organizations that could offer these types of roles, as well as the skills, knowledge, experience, and education needed for such positions.

_____

_____

---

9. Define your company criteria.

This step is the last in your Internal Assessment. I have included this step to help you develop the list of criteria that you feel is most important to you. As you develop your job search strategy, you should use the list you develop as your criteria in identifying those companies that you want to work for. These companies will be your target companies. Use the following questions to help define your company criteria.

- What are the most important attributes of your target companies? Examples might include:

  Financially stable

  Public

  International

  Technology focused

  Strong customers

  Strong leadership

  Culturally stable

  Strong employee orientation program

Once you have completed your Internal Assessment, take a thirty-minute break to clear your head.

The next step is for you to complete an External Assessment. The External Assessment is designed to help you think about the possible resources you can use to research target companies. The External Assessment should also help you formulate your job search strategy and provide a framework to follow during your quest for your new job.

External Assessment

1. To begin your research, identify fifteen target companies that match your company criteria.

Develop a list of target companies for which you are interested in working. As you consider these companies, match each company to your list of important attributes that you developed during the Internal Assessment. Is location important to you? If so, your target companies might be in the same geographic region. Are you interested in a specific industry or specific company size?

The most important aspect of this exercise is to force you to narrow your search to fifteen target companies. This exercise will help you focus on those companies that interest you. Notice that I have not asked you if your target companies have open positions. At this point of your job search, identifying target companies that match your criteria is more important than looking only at those companies that are currently hiring. Industries change, job markets fluctuate, and companies' hiring schedules differ by month. As you begin researching companies, you might find that companies drop off the list, which will require you to add more names. In general, a better approach is to focus your time and energies on target companies that match your criteria than applying a shotgun approach to a job search, only to become frustrated very early in the process.

1. _____

2. _____

3. _____

4. _____

5. _____

6. _____

7. _____

8. _____

9. _____

10. _____

11. _____

12. _____

13. _____

14. _____

15. _____

2. Identify the best resources to research the target companies.

Start building your list of resources to research your fifteen target companies. These resources could be personal referrals from your network of contacts, corporate Web sites, career centers, trade journals, annual reports, and so on. Later in this book, we highlight multiple resources that you can use. However, for this assessment, I want you to identify those resources that you are currently aware of and to which you have access.

_____

_____

_____

_____

3. Determine the type of information you need.

As you prepare to research each target company, develop a template to follow during your research. This template should highlight the most important information you need to gather during your job search. This assessment is the starting point, but as you read more of this book, this list of questions will grow. The following is a sample list of questions.

- What industry is the company in?

- How large is the company?

- Who are its competitors?

- What type of products/services does the company produce/provide?

- Who are the company's customers/prospects?

- What type of culture does the company promote?

- What type of benefits does the company promote?

- What criteria does the company look for when hiring?

4. Develop a plan to conduct your research.

Now that you have developed a list of fifteen target companies, identified resources to conduct your company research, and developed your research template, you need to create a plan of action. As you begin, make sure to include organizational processes such as filing methods and written or electronic documentation of your findings. Your research needs to be easily assessable and understandable later in the process. You need to stay organized and focused on learning as much about each company as you can. This plan should also include a timeline and specific milestones to measure your success. How much time should you spend to research each target company? What is your timeline to find a job? What will be your weekly milestones of success during this search? In my experience, I found that many hiring managers and recruiters selected those candidates who did their research and understood the organization.

As you develop your job search strategy, think about the types of companies for which you would like to work. You should develop a criteria list before you start your research.

Many people place value on many different aspects of an organization. A sample list of criteria that you might consider follows. This list was developed through a series of focus groups and organizational surveys as well as candidate interviews. The criteria are organized into specific categories, including general company criteria, cultural requirements, leadership expectations, career growth, compensation and benefits, and community involvement. Identify your most valued criteria and use it as a benchmark for your target companies.

General Company Criteria

Organizational stability

Financial stability

Solid organizational history and future direction

Industry recognition

Community recognition

Quality products and services

Location

Office environment

Cultural diversity

Organizational values

Ethics/honesty

Morale and social environment

Teamwork and collaboration

Cultural Requirements

Documented orientation and assimilation program

Work-life balance

Flexibility

Healthy and social environment

Collaboration and teamwork

Competence of peers

Equipment and productivity tools

Reward and recognition system

Family orientation

Standard market benefits (such as vacation and personal time)

Well-documented policies and procedures

Opportunity to contribute

High employee morale

Solid company communication process and practice

Leadership Expectation

Visionary leadership

Solid leader/employee relations

Communication skills

Individual respect

Ability to coach and provide feedback

Follow-through and time management

Ability to adapt to change

Accountability

Emotional intelligence

Self-awareness	Self-regulation
Motivation	Empathy
Social skills	

Career Growth

Individual career development plans

Documented monitoring program

Documented feedback and performance evaluation system

Solid education and training

Support for higher education

Cross-training opportunities

Documented job descriptions and position specifications

Clear process for promotions and/or transfers

Opportunity to tutor and/or mentor others

Compensation and Benefits

Competitive base salary

Performance-based compensation program

Realistic bonus opportunities

Stock/profit-sharing program

Group health insurance program

Dental/vision insurance

Life and accidental death insurance

Short-term and long-term disability coverage

Paid holidays/vacation/sick days

Tuition and training reimbursement

Community Involvement

Cultural events

Social conscience

Philanthropic involvement

Charity contributions

Volunteerism

Now that you have completed the Internal Assessment and the External Assessment, it is time to document your job search strategy. Figure 1 is an actual job search strategy document that one of my clients developed. His job search strategy was about five pages long and included much more information that he used to find his job. I am happy to say that he found a job within forty-eight days of completing his Internal Assessment, External Assessment, and job search strategy document. Obviously, results vary, but a well-documented job search strategy can greatly improve your success, motivation, and overall focus.

Figure 1

Job Search Strategy Example

Internal Assessment
Define your personal and professional goals.

Personal:

What types of jobs motivate you?

I am motivated by technology and am interested in a job where I can be creative as well as use my ability to work in a collaborative team environment.

Where do you want to live now and in the future?

I want to stay in the Chicago area.

What type of job would make you happy?

I am interested in a marketing role in a software development company.

Professional:

What type of company would you like to work for?

I want to work for a software development company in Chicago.

What type of starting salary are you expecting?

My salary expectation is $85,000 per year.

Are you planning to get an MBA, MS, or specific certifications?

I want to find a firm that has a strong tuition reimbursement program that will help fund an MBA.

What type of company environment do you desire?

I would like to work for a small private firm where I can wear many hats and learn about the business from various perspectives. I want to be a big fish in a small pond.

What type of boss/manager motivates you?

I am motivated by a manager who is knowledgeable about the business and my role and will help coach and mentor me to reach my career goals.

Set your career target.

Where do you want to be in 5 or 10 years?

I want to be a vice president of marketing in a software company.

Define the possible steps that will help you attain your career target.

What type of company would align with your career target?

I need to work for a small software company that is market driven and has senior-level marketing support.

What type of education will you need to have?

I need an MBA as well as professional certifications such as in Pragmatic Marketing.

What type of professional experience will you need to acquire to reach your career target?

I need to acquire marketing experience in technology marketing, product marketing, company positioning, marketing communications, marketing research, and sales support.

Define your company criteria.

What are the most important attributes of your target companies?

I need to find a company that is market driven and provides an opportunity to learn and grow.

What criteria should your target companies possess?

My target companies need to be software development companies in Chicago.

My target companies need to provide a learning environment and focus on career development of their people.

My target companies need to be team oriented and collaborative so that I can learn from others and provide my feedback if needed.

My target companies need to have strong software products that align with specific industries.

My target companies need to be financially stable, have strong employment stability, and have a strong culture.

What type of company would have your target positions?

Most software development companies that are members of the Chicago Software Association have marketing positions within the firm.

External Assessment

Identify 15 companies that match your company criteria to begin your research.

I have conducted some research for Chicago-based software development firms on Chicago Software Association's Web site (CSA.org) and found 15 target companies that match my criteria.

Identify your resources to research the target companies.

What resource should you use to conduct your research?

I have a strong network in the marketing field.

I plan to use the job boards such as Monster.com and Careerbuilder.com.

I plan to use the Internet to research my target companies through associations such as CSA.org and Society for Information Management. Once I have their names, I will visit and study their Web sites.

I plan to use the Naperville Career Center to help with my search.

I plan to contact each target firm to conduct an informational interview.

Determine the type of information you need.

I feel all of these questions need to be answered and documented as part of my research.

- *What industries does the company market to?*

- *How large is the company?*

- *Who are its competitors?*

- *What type of products does the company produce/provide?*

- *Who are the company's customers/prospects?*

- *How do you define the target company's culture?*

- *What criteria does the company look for when hiring?*

Develop a strategy to contact the company to set up an interview.

How should you prioritize your target companies?

- *I need to research each of these 15 and then prioritize those companies based on:*

  - *My network's knowledge.*

  - *Open positions posted.*

  - *Any past experience or competitive advantage I may have.*

How much time should you spend to research each target company?

- *I plan to spend one day just researching each company.*

- *I will develop a schedule for each day as well as document my findings based on the previous criteria that I have listed as important.*

- *I will identify specific milestones such as two interviews per week, five résumés and cover letters sent per day, and six hours per day spent researching target companies.*

- *I will provide my schedule to my wife to motivate me to stay on track and focus.*

What is your timeline to find a job?

• *My goal is to find a job in 90 days.*

Use the Internal and External Assessments as your guide to help you finalize your job search strategy and use your time as efficiently as possible.

This book references often the value of research. The more time you spend up front researching an organization and market data, the better the end results will be. Let me provide a real example. When I was recruiting for two open positions in my company, I found two similar candidates with the same educational background as well as the same type of work experience. One of the candidates was named Ben and the other was named Susan. Both candidates were well educated with bachelor degrees, extracurricular activities, backgrounds, and experiences. The position that they were interviewing for had an average salary range of $35,000 to $42,000. The small position posting on the Internet gave some company details and skill expectations as well as a starting salary of $35,000. The posting also had a link to our Web site, which provided more extensive knowledge about my company.

The first interview was with Ben. I asked him a series of standard interview questions such as, "Why should I hire you?" "What are your strengths and weaknesses?" and "What are your career goals and objectives?" Then I asked some very revealing questions such as "Tell me about my company." and "What are your salary expectations?"

Ben answered the standard questions very well, and I was very impressed. However, when it came to the specific questions about my company and salary expectations, Ben obviously did not do his homework. He told me that my company was in the software business and that we were international. These were fine answers that he read in the job posting. When I asked him if he visited my Web site, he said that he briefly reviewed the site but could not recall any specific information regarding our business model, office locations, or product line. I also asked him about his salary expectations, and he explained that the salary range posted was fine. Although I did not feel Ben spent much time researching my organization, I was impressed with his background and was planning to offer him the job.

When I interviewed the second candidate, Susan, I asked the same type of questions. Susan's answers were very good. I felt she was also very qualified for the job. When it came to the company and salary questions, Susan was much more prepared. She explained that my company had eight products and sold into four major industries. She told me we were international with ten global offices, and she proceeded to list some of our customers in each industry. I could tell she did her homework. When it came to the salary questions, Susan was also prepared. Her opening statement was, "Based on my research, I found that this position requires strong communication skills and technical knowledge as well as customer service experience. Based on these skills and the market value of the open position, which is $35,000 to $45,000, I am looking for a starting salary of $43,000 per year." Again, she mentioned that these figures were based on her research.

I hired both candidates. We paid Ben $35,000 and paid Susan $43,000. I am not suggesting that every company will match your salary requirements; she was right about the market value for the position, and I did not want to lose her as a candidate. From the very first day, Susan's salary was at a much stronger position than Ben's because of her understanding of the market and her extensive research. Make sure you spend time researching the company as well as the position's skill requirements and compensation figures. The job search process is like a sporting event. The person who has done the most planning, preparation, and practice has the best odds of success.

In summary, as you begin your job search, you should plan a solid course of action. Conduct an Internal Assessment to identify what motivates you and the types of environments that will help you thrive. Also conduct an External Assessment to help identify the possible resources you should use to identify and research target companies. You should identify fifteen companies that match your criteria and spend approximately one full day per company gathering as much information as possible. This information helps you develop a targeted résumé, interview questions, and interview answers.

As you plan your job search strategy, use this book to help identify additional resources you can use. The chapters walk you through the process of an informational interview and help you identify proper interview attire, prepare for the interview, and negotiate your starting salary. Finally, this book helps you succeed in your new position by providing an outline of specific organizational areas that help you thrive with your new employer.

Chapter 2

Resources

"A single conversation across the table with a wise man
is worth a month's study of books."
Chinese proverb

Now that you have completed your Internal and External Assessments, it is time to identify those resources that are available to aid you in the employment process. This chapter highlights various resources you can use to research companies, to learn more about specific industries or occupations, or to find open positions. Whether you are a recent college grad or an experienced professional looking to make a career or job change, these resources can be invaluable tools to finding the job you want.

Career Center (Community or University)
Many universities as well as community centers offer a type of career center or a place to conduct research and help guide you through your job search. If you are currently a college student or recent graduate, the career center at your college or university is a great place to start. If you are not a college student, you should check with your local chamber of commerce or city hall to obtain information on local community career centers. Most towns have some sort of community career center that is available to residents. Even a local library

could serve as a good starting point for conducting research.

Career centers can offer a variety of resources to help point you in the right direction for your job search. One important tool that many career centers offer is an aptitude or compatibility evaluation, which is basically an assessment (similar to what you have just completed in the last chapter) that is designed to match up your interests with industries or job positions according to your personality or career goals. The evaluation results can then be used to identify what types of companies or industries you should consider researching. Most career centers have counselors available to assist you in this process or give career options.

Once you have an idea of what industry or field interests you and you have developed your target list of potential employers, you can take advantage of the multitude of informational resources available at the career center. Whether contained in books or on electronic databases, resources at career centers should include:

- Industry information.

- Listings of companies within specific fields and where they are located.

- Salary guides such as Mercer, Watson Wyatt, or Culpepper. These guides typically segment the market by industry, position title, description, and geographic locations. Make sure the information is from a credible source.

- Industry outlook (for example, what industries are expected to need the most employees now and in the future).

- Resources such as Hoovers.com, Dun and Bradstreet, or Leadership Library in order for you to conduct company research (what the company does, how they are doing financially, who their competitors are, etc.).

- Information and examples for effective résumé and cover letter development.

• Dedicated career counselors to answer questions, teach interview and résumé workshops, and provide private offices to conduct your phone interviews.

Many career centers have computer software programs available so you can complete a résumé electronically. In addition, the career center likely has a database of current open positions you can search. In many cases, you can submit your résumé electronically for positions that interest you. In addition, they probably have a contact list for various local companies or companies that frequent the center to recruit new hires.

> *Tip: When conducting company research, check to see when the company's fiscal year ends. Most companies have tight budgets at the end of a fiscal year but have an influx of budgetary monies in the early part of the fiscal year. Therefore, a good approach is to plan your job search for the early part of a company's fiscal year.*

Network

Your network is another resource that can be used for finding a job. In my experience, nearly 70 percent of all successful job acquisitions began with networking. In addition, the majority of human resource professionals, recruiters, and hiring managers prefer to hire someone they know or have met through a referral from their network. So, what is networking and how can you make it work for you?

Networking often refers to a social activity typically utilizing reciprocal relationships to facilitate communication between people. In addition, there are different strategies, techniques, and motivations behind networking. Networking can be a very powerful tool to building skills and capabilities and acquiring access to opportunities and information. Networking is actually a fairly simple process; you just need to know where to start. Here are the basic steps to begin.

Step 1: Make a list of all of your personal contacts that you may need to leverage during the job search. Include your peers, professors, parents, brothers, sisters, roommates, or anyone who might be able to give you a tip about a company, a job, or some connection associated with the company. Make sure this list includes contact information such as phone numbers, e-mail addresses, and so on.

Step 2: Segment your personal network list into subgroups such as school, work, church, professional organizations, and social organizations. A good way to do this is to have each contact listed on a three-by-five-inch index card or in an electronic database.

> *Tip: Purchase for your personal computer an electronic database or contact software tool such as ACT. This database allows you to enter contact names, search by contact information, and provide detailed notes about each contact conversation. This tool is one that grows as your career grows.*

Step 3: Develop a script for each segment in your network, highlighting what you plan to say during the conversation. In writing the different scripts, consider the type of job you are looking for and the types of companies you are interested in.

> Example: "Hello, John, during our conversation last week, you mentioned that you knew a friend at XYZ Company who was looking for a product manager for the Midwest division. Currently, I am looking for a new job and would be very interested in learning more about that opportunity. In fact, in my last position, I was the product manager for DEF product line, which is XYZ's largest competitor. Could I reference you when I call your friend? Thanks for your help."

> Example: "Hello, Sue, last Sunday after church you

mentioned that you knew of a career networking group that met at church every Saturday morning. As you know, I am looking for a new job in the field of marketing and would be very interested in attending with you. Would that be okay? Thanks, and I will see you on Saturday."

Step 4: Develop a game plan to contact your network via letter, e-mail, phone call, and/or meeting. Within this plan, you might consider developing a message or announcement that could be sent to your network. I recommend contacting your network first with your message and then sending them a copy of your résumé if they are interested. Remember the six degrees of separation. Your network has a network that has a network of people that have common interests. One often hears that we are all connected by only six degrees of separation. You never know who and where you might find your next lead. Use this plan to help communicate your efforts and goals of your job search to your broad network of contacts.

Your goal list to begin your networking should resemble the following:

- Finalize my résumé and cover letter by January.

- Develop a letter that informs my personal network of my intention to find a new job as well as highlights some of my skills and attributes.

- Distribute an e-mail to my close personal network.

- Send a finalized résumé and cover letter to people who show interest.

- Call and schedule lunch with my top-five business colleagues.

- Acquire the schedule for the Chicago Software Association's next networking event and schedule time to attend.

Once you have compiled your personal network list, begin to make contact (by phone, e-mail, etc.) and see what names or contacts your personal network can provide. As you gather networking names, create a card catalog using index cards (or the electronic database) with the person's name, phone number, occupation, and any other important information you may need to use later—especially the person who gave you the contact name. Make sure you also record personal data such as number of children, hometown, favorite sports teams, and so on. Be sure to save this card catalog. You may contact these names years later and find out that some may be in a position to hire you.

In addition to your personal contacts, you can expand your network by joining various organizations, such as industry-specific organizations or even community or church organizations. While industry-specific organizations are more likely to produce job opportunities in your chosen career field, you never know where you might hear about open positions. Many churches are developing networking groups that support each other, network, and provide advice. Check with your church or those in your community to learn more.

Yet another important way to network is to attend functions where professionals in your field will be in attendance and/or giving a presentation (trade shows, industry conferences, meetings, and small-group gatherings). These forums offer good opportunities to establish a contact in an organization and to learn more about the company, what it does, and its prospects for the future. Try to meet the speaker personally if possible. For instance, if a representative of a company is giving a speech, try to approach the speaker afterwards and discuss the speech, the company, or common interests. Be sure to introduce yourself and get the person's business card if you can. When networking, the objective is to become connected and known to the people who have hiring authority.

Let's assume you are attending a trade organization meeting for an industry in which you wish to work. Here are some tips to keep in mind when you are networking for career purposes:

Identify your strengths and the value you have to offer. What are your greatest strengths? Convert those strengths into a value that you would offer a company or employer. In every interview I ask, "What can you do for us?" You need to identify the value that you bring and phrase it in terms of return on investment (ROI). If the company invests in you, what benefit will it receive in return?

Identify the types of opportunities you are targeting. Match your strengths to these types of opportunities or positions. What makes you unique to fill a particular job?

Create your marketing message. Utilize the strengths you've identified to develop a short verbal business card or personal commercial. Here's an example: "As a sales rep for Tech Systems, I focused on industry knowledge, developing relationships, and growing revenue. My industry knowledge helped develop a list of forty qualified prospects. My relationship skills opened the doors to meet decision-makers and executive-level contacts and to identify potential solutions to their problems. In fact, the result is an average annual revenue increase of 48 percent over the past twelve months, at a time when the industry is experiencing a significant recession."

> *Tip: Smile, be personable, look people in the eye, and show your interest by asking questions and (most importantly) listening to their responses.*

Plan, plan, plan. If you are attending a large event, make sure you develop a game plan to cover all the ground efficiently. Identify the list of attendees whom you want to meet, including potential times and locations. Ask your personal network for recommendations on whom you should consider meeting. If possible, do some homework on the company and/or specific contact. In some cases, it may be appropriate to e-mail or phone your contact or scheduled speakers in advance of the event. Mention that you'll be attending and looking forward to introducing yourself.

Track your progress. Make sure you measure your networking success by the number of meaningful conversations you've had. Make sure you focus on the conversation and the people you are meeting, not just the fact that you are looking for a job.

Understand your contact's needs. Make sure you understand your contact's needs so you can understand how you can be of value. Develop a list of intelligent questions: What type of projects are you currently working on? Is there any need for help with this specific project? Are you are looking to hire people with any specific skills? I noticed from my research that your company was merging with XYZ; how will that affect these projects you are tasked with? What resources or ideas are you looking for at this event?

If you are not a fit for that company's needs, you may want to provide a referral of someone from your personal network.

Remember your marketing theme and match it to the contact's needs. You want to be in a place to position yourself as the answer to the needs of your targeted companies. For instance, "In my most recent position, we had to solve the same problem. In fact, my role was to . . ."

Continue to build your network. Make sure you capitalize on the opportunity to ask for a business card and/or permission to make contact again soon. However, be ever conscious of nonverbal behavior. If they are looking at their watch or looking around the room, use that time to say, "I do not want to take too much of your time. Could I get your business card and maybe we can finish our discussion after the conference?"

> *Tip: There is a standard etiquette to receiving a business card. When someone hands you his or her card, make sure you read the person's name out loud. People always like hearing their own name, and it shows that you have interest and appreciate their card. Then, once they leave, turn the card over and write specific characteristics about the meeting or conversation on the back of the card. You should document appearance, such*

*as "blond hair, tall, black coat" to help refresh
your memory.*

You should also document some facts about the conversation. For instance, "Talked about the Cleveland Indians" and "Found out that they will be converting their systems and need a project manager." The point of this exercise is to provide a refresher so that you will remember the person three months from now.

In fact, on my desk at my office, I have a plastic recipe box with business cards taped to index cards. On every card is a description of the person as well as their role and details about our last conversation. I have segmented the cards by industry as well as job function. I use this manual network filing system on a monthly basis to stay in touch with my close contacts. This process can also be automated with the use of a personal electronic address or contact tool.

Final thought on networking. Be yourself and take an honest interest in others. Be a good listener to the concerns of your network. Help them solve their problems or meet other contacts so that they want to help you when the time comes. Networking is a reciprocal relationship. The more you care about others, the more you will succeed.

Internet

The most accessible research vehicle is the Internet. I could spend the entire book just discussing strategies that you can use with the Internet to conduct extensive research on industries, positions, companies, salaries, and anything else. However, because of the focus of this book, I will keep it brief. The Internet can be a very powerful tool if you know how and where to look for information. Here are some general suggestions:

Company Web sites

Once you have identified companies that you think match your career goals, the best place to start is the Web site for the individual company. These sites generally contain basic information about the company, such as what it does, what products it sells or makes, how long it has been in business, and where it is located. The sites may also contain information on the broader industry and the company's ranking within the industry (if applicable).

Publicly traded companies usually have an investor relations section that provides financial information on the company. If they don't, you can look this information up on the Edgar database on the SEC's Web site (www.sec.gov), which focuses on public companies. Other information on a company's site probably includes press releases, customer testimonials, or other marketing information. Many companies also have open job positions listed on their Web sites. You can often search for open jobs and even apply right online to many of these.

Job boards

Job boards are online listings of open positions. A wide variety of job boards appear on the Internet. Some of the most popular include www.monster.com, www.headhunter.net, www.employmentspot.com, www.dice.com, www.jobs.com, and www.careerbuilder.com. Some job boards are dedicated to a specific industry, such as software and technology, manufacturing, retail, and nursing, to name a few. In addition, some sites are geographically focused, posting jobs only for specific areas such as the East Coast or Chicago. With the ever-changing Internet career board marketplace, I recommend using a search engine such as Yahoo or Google to search for job boards.

Once you have found a job board, you can easily search for open positions by location, job title, key words, or company. Most of the job boards also allow you to post your résumé and apply for open jobs online. While some of you may fear having too much information about yourself out on public display, there are ways to keep some privacy when posting your résumé. If you are concerned about a current employer seeing your résumé on a job board, don't list your company. Instead, just give the description of the firm. For instance, instead of saying ABC Corporation, say "a Fortune 500 software development firm with sales in excess of $1 billion." In addition, your e-mail address should be a confidential one, not your work e-mail address.

Professional association/organization Web sites

In addition to your target company's Web site, job boards, or search engines, I also recommend visiting sites focused on professional associations and organizations. These Web sites often contain valuable industry information such as articles or newsletters as well as potential employment opportunities.

Other sites

Many other resources are available online to assist you in your career endeavors. Most newspapers now have online versions of their classified ads. Check out these types of sites for online job listings specific to a target city or state. Local government sites or chambers of commerce tend to have Web sites that may have links to open positions within the community as well. Search engines can also lead you to other valuable information such as salary guides or cost of living comparisons. These types of sites can be very helpful when considering a job for which you would be relocating to another part of the country. The key to successfully navigating your way through the Internet is to be creative, patient, and relentless.

Professional Organizations

Involvement in professional organizations or associations is another resource for your job search. If you are already a member of a professional organization, I recommend becoming involved in roundtable discussions and events, committees, task forces, and monthly networking events. These places are all great for meeting people and networking with like-minded individuals. If you are not involved with any professional organizations, get involved. Locate an industry organization that best suits you and apply for membership. Once you are a member, become involved. You can network and socialize while you learn more about your industry and chosen profession and also learn about open positions, meet hiring managers, and investigate companies or organizations.

Professional Recruiting Firms

If you have been working for five or more years, you should begin to add professional recruiters into your job search strategy. Until you have five years of work experience, most qualified and reputable recruiting firms will not consider you as a truly viable candidate.

Before jumping into the details and guidelines for working with recruiting firms, let me make this important point. Spend no more than 10 percent of your total job search time with recruiters. Do not fall into a common trap that you've got a great recruiter who is going to find a job for you. Recruiters do not make money by finding you a job. They earn their money by finding specific people for their clients—the company or organization that hires them to do this work.

Let's start with a brief overview. The two different types of professional recruiting firms are contingency and retained. (Knowing this fact is not going to modify your approach, but I want you to look well informed as you begin to approach these professionals.) Contingency recruiting firms are paid only when their client (company) hires someone whom the recruiter brings. Retained search firms are paid to be the exclusive search firm for a specific position. The assumption is that they will work on the search until they find a person who pleases the client. It most situations, retained search firms are typically used for senior-level positions, those with salary ranges from $100,000 and up.

From a networking perspective, I would encourage you to spend some time taking several steps to maximize your reach within this segment of your total network. First, conduct some research to identify a list of recruiting firms that you want to know you. Just like your search for target employer prospects, doing some upfront work can pay off handsomely in the end.

- Find firms that specialize in your profession. Some firms focus on just accounting or information technology. Make sure you are targeting those firms that handle the career track you want to pursue.

- Find firms that have strong visibility in your city or in the nation if you are open to relocation.

Once you have assembled your list of these firms, the next step is to contact each firm with the following objectives in mind:

- Confirm that this firm is interested in having you in its database. Do your best to ascertain that it has had business and is continuing to have business placing people like yourself.

- Ask if someone would be interested in meeting with you in person. If the firm is open to this, I believe it is a good sign that the company will do a better job in representing you and working for its clients.

- Whether in person or over the phone, spend some time with people of the firm. You want to make sure that a few key things happen:

  - Your résumé gets into their database.

  - All the contact information about yourself is entered correctly.

  - They understand the specific types of jobs you are both interested in and qualified for. Depending on your experience and capabilities, a variety of positions might be appropriate. Most sophisticated databases can handle a person with multiple job preferences, but you need to make sure that the people entering your information into the database understand this. Some newer database systems allow you to enter your own information via the Web. I strongly recommend you do this. That way you can tailor your profile exactly the way you want and ensure that your multiple job positions are accurately represented.

- Finally, take some time to chat with the people in these firms:

  - What are the market conditions; what's hot and what's not? What companies are hiring? What types of positions are being filled? You can learn a lot about the current hiring climate from professionals who make their living finding people for companies who are paying significant sums of money to hire new employees.

  - Ask them to critique your résumé. Again, you are on the phone or having coffee with people who earn their living reading résumés, interviewing people, and making decisions on whom to present to their clients based on those two activities. They truly are professionals in an arena where you need help. So, while you have their attention, benefit from their experience and opinions.

  - Thank them for their time and keep in touch with those whom you felt were truly professional and personable. Even after you find your next job, remember that your job-hunting days will come again.

Now that you've identified quality recruiting firms that focus on the same positions and industries as yourself—and you've taken the time to meet them, get into their databases, and listen to their suggestions—you can put that part of your job search on the back burner. Remember, only 10 percent of your job search time should be spent with recruiters. Following the steps I've suggested has put you ahead of 90 percent of the rest of the job hunters in the eyes and databases of professional recruiters. If you want to put yourself ahead of 99 percent of the job hunters in the recruiters' world, take the step that will dramatically improve your networking results: Ask how you can help them! You probably know someone in your network who would like to be linked to a very good, pre-qualified professional recruiting firm. If you've already done the legwork, research, and qualification, then you have a valuable piece of information that you should use. Bring together someone in your network with the best recruiting firm or recruiter that you have now uncovered. I can guarantee that taking this step will put you ahead of 99 percent of the other candidates in that recruiter's list. Helping others who you would like help from always increases your chances of success. It's as simple as the Golden Rule.

> *Tip: For those of you with fewer than five years of work experience, I do not mean to state unequivocally that you should not work with or accept opportunities from professional recruiting firms. Companies sometimes engage the services of contingency firms to conduct searches that may include people in your segment, but these types of searches are rare. If a recruiting firm contacts you, go ahead and follow through with them. I would just suggest that you not make working and networking with recruiting firms a part of your overall job search campaign until you have at least five years of work experience.*

Staffing and Temporary Firms

Understanding this segment of the world of business and how to work effectively within it is becoming increasingly important in any good job campaign. Whether the company is called a temporary personnel firm, a staffing firm, or a contracting firm, with all of them you are legally employed by that firm and will be working at a client's office for that firm. We cover more of the details shortly, but here are some important statistics to understand about this growing segment of our workforce.

According to the Bureau of Labor Statistics more than 3 million people will be employed in the personnel supply industry by 2006, and the expected annual growth rate of almost 10 percent makes this industry one of the fastest growing in the economy.

The most common category of temporary workers is administrative and clerical support occupations. However, professionals, including engineering, managerial, and computer workers, now make up over 11 percent of the personnel supply services industry. Growth in demand for these skilled occupations is expected to outpace the growth in demand for temporary clerical positions.

Let me explain why a company would choose to hire a staffing firm to bring people to them, instead of just hiring the people directly.

It only needs the help for a project or a period of time. Many times companies have projects that have a specific beginning and ending date. Hiring a new full-time employee would not make sense, so it engages the services of a staffing firm to provide that specific talent for that specific length of time. Also, a company might have extra work because of a person being on a medical leave or just unable to do their normal job, again creating the need for some specific help for a period of time.

The company needs something accomplished, and it lacks specific expertise. A new computer system is being installed, a new product is ready for market, or employees need to be trained on some new systems or tools. The reasons are many, but the solution is common. "Bring in someone who can help us get over this hump!"

The company is not sure they really need a new full-time person, so it hires a temporary worker first. As companies grow, they often feel the need to increase the employee head count. Bringing on new employees first as a contract employee can allow the company to test drive the person's abilities and allow the company to better understand the impact on the business. In this way, the company can determine if the increase in head count is the right solution while providing a way for the company to determine how well that new person fits into its environment.

Now that you have a better understanding of why companies use staffing firms and temporary employees, you can see how working with these firms can increase your pathways to success in your job campaign. Companies need people, just not always people that they employ. The image of temporary workers doing repetitive, low-skilled work is as outdated as black-and-white television. So, if you feel as though joining the ranks of the temporary workforce is beneath you, you are missing out on a huge segment of the future workforce. Whether you are directly out of college or have thirty-five years of work experience, joining companies in this method can be just as profitable and rewarding as being a full-time employee.

As with all the other aspects of your job search campaign, working for a staffing firm also starts with research. You need to find the staffing firms in your niche that focus on the type of work you are seeking. If you are a recent graduate and looking for an entry-level accounting, marketing, or advertising job, there are staffing firms that specialize in these categories. In fact, for those of you who are still unsure about your career plans, landing a position with a staffing firm may be just the ticket for exploring different types of industries and careers. I have seen several firms hire people fresh from college to handle very responsible positions that involved helping major corporations roll out new systems or introduce new products. These types of projects can involve a variety of responsibilities, heavy travel, and high visibility within the corporate headquarters. What a great way to start your career!

If you are well into your career and looking to make a change or are forced to make a change, staffing or contract opportunities are a great way to bridge the gap between those stages in your career. Find staffing firms that work with experienced people in your industry. Regardless of your profession, temporary staffing is a viable and growing segment of our workforce.

Find those staffing or contracting firms that deal with people like you. Introduce yourself to them, just like you would to a recruiting firm. Whether over the phone or in person, make sure they know who you are, what abilities you have, and what you can do. Make sure your résumé is in their databases. Are you willing to travel? Are you willing to work forty hours a week? What is your desired hourly wage? As with your favorite recruiters, keep in touch and follow the Golden Rule! Maybe someone in your network could benefit from being linked to a pre-qualified staffing or contracting company. Connecting your preferred staffing or contracting professional to a new potential customer puts you ahead of 99 percent of the other potential candidates in that professional's database.

Print Media

Another resource you can use for your research is print media: newspapers, magazines, and journals. In some industries, newspaper employment advertisements are still a popular method that employers use to find prospective candidates. As part of your search, you should review your local newspaper or the newspaper in the geographic area you are targeting and review the employment advertisements. In addition, review the stories in the newspaper regarding your target companies. Understanding the most current events regarding your target companies might be very useful.

Magazines are also very useful for company research. Some magazines target specific industries while other magazines focus on private companies or public companies. There are magazines that list the "Best Places to Work" and "The Most Family-Friendly Work Environment" or "Employers of Choice." Some magazines have the top one hundred or five hundred companies in America for both private and public industry. Review these magazines to learn more about the companies you are targeting.

Informational Interview

Another resource you could use for your job search is the informational interview. An informational interview is used primarily for two reasons: to gather more information about a company and to gather more information about a specific job. Whether you are just out of college or have fifteen years of experience, informational interviews are a valuable process in validating your career choice and conducting an effective job campaign.

An informational interview begins with a phone call to the prospective companies or people you have researched. Develop a script of the phone call before you call. The script should have everything you want to say to the company. This script should also include blank sections for questions and answers you might discuss during the call. Make sure you study this script and know what you are going to say before your call. However, don't read your script word for word. Nothing is worse than having someone recite a script to you on the phone. Just have a general idea of what you want to say and make sure the script is available as a reference. An example of this script appears on the following page.

The first person you contact will likely be the receptionist. He or she should be your first friend in the company. I have found through my research that the coordinator or receptionist plays a large part in the hiring process. They are often asked questions about a candidate's phone etiquette and personality. Often they are asked to give their general opinion of the applicants they speak with on the telephone and in person. Therefore, begin selling your skills to this person while gaining valuable information about the company. Make sure you learn his or her name and try to establish a rapport. Get the spelling of their name if you need it, and write down the person's name on your informational interview script.

The best way to start the conversation with the receptionist is to ask for help.

> *You: Hello, whom am I speaking with? My name is*
> *_____; I am currently attending Florida*
> *State University and am doing research on XYZ Corp.*
> *In this research I am required to contact the accounting*
> *manager (or the department you are interested in).*
> *Could you please give me some guidance?*
>
> *Receptionist: Sure, whom would you like to talk with?*
>
> *You: I am not sure. I would like to see if it is possible*
> *to schedule a fifteen-minute meeting with this person.*
> *Who would you recommend?*
>
> *Receptionist: I am sorry; I am not allowed to provide*
> *names over the phone. I will just put you though to the*
> *accounting department. Is that okay?*
>
> *You: Sure, Barbara. Thanks very much for your time.*

Say the same thing to this coordinator in the accounting department as you did to the receptionist. Asking for help and asking questions allows you to gather information as well as allow the coordinator to feel that he/she is important and helpful to you. Remember that the receptionist's role is to be a gatekeeper. Receptionists are required to screen every call and only let the important calls through. Make your call sound very important.

If the receptionist does not put you through to the accounting manager, which is your final goal, the receptionist may want to take your name and have someone call you back. Give the receptionist your name and begin to ask more questions.

> *You: Would it be okay to send this person a letter? If*
> *so, to whom do I send it?*

At this point, with any luck you can get the name and contact the person directly. If not, then explain to the receptionist exactly what your meeting is regarding. This step will be your final plea to get the accounting manager's name.

> *You: I understand, maybe you can help me. I am graduating from Florida State University with a bachelor of arts in accounting. I am conducting research on your company, because I am very interested in working with you. I just wanted to see if it would be possible to meet with someone in your accounting department to give me detailed information about your team. Is there anyone in your accounting department whom I could talk with?*

At this point, they may put you through to someone in the accounting department or try to put you through to human resources or recruiting. When you are talking with the recruiter, give the same speech that you gave to the receptionist. One thing you will quickly learn in your career is that you need to have contingency or secondary plans prepared. Your goal is to put yourself in front of people who can help you. Whether you succeed with the recruiter or the accounting manager, any contact in a company is very important.

Another option is dialing for names. Dialing for names involves a phone, the main number at the company, and your guts. Let's just say that the company's phone number is (555) 540-5000. Chances are that the company's extensions are also in the 5000s. Just begin dialing for names by dialing (555) 540-5001. When a person picks up, just politely explain that you must have dialed the wrong number and simply ask if they can transfer you to the accounting department. This technique does not always work, but just give it a shot. You have nothing to lose.

Now, let's say you have been connected with the human resources manager or accounting department. Remember that this recruiter is only thinking about his current openings in the company and not your future at the company. Make sure you respect the person's time! Recruiters are very busy and tend to focus on their positions at hand. However, they know everything about the company and could help answer your questions if needed. If you reach the accounting department, remember that they are also very busy. Reveal your interests in the company and your purpose for the phone call. They might ask you to send in a résumé. Sure, send them a résumé. You have done your research and you have seen the company's Web site. Try to build your résumé around some of the company's values before you send it to the recruiter.

> You: *"Hello, my name is_____. Do you have a moment to talk? I am preparing to graduate from Florida State University in accounting and am beginning my job search process. I have done some research on XYZ Corp., and I am interested in learning more about your company. I am conducting informational interviews with the companies in which I am interested and would be honored if I could schedule a fifteen-minute appointment with you to ask five questions about XYZ Corp. as well as the accounting and finance group."*

Or

> *"Hello Mr. Black, my name is Tim Augustine. Jim Butler gave me your name, and I would like to ask a favor of you. I am interested in a career similar to yours. It would mean a lot to me if I could have the opportunity to meet with you in your office to ask some questions and maybe even get your advice regarding my career. If you are open to this, when could we schedule a meeting that would be convenient for you?"*

The key to this interview is to build a business friendship. Remember that your goal is to gather information about the company. If you set up an informational interview with a recruiter or the accounting manager, make sure you utilize this time to gather as much data as you can.

After you contact each company and schedule an appointment, prepare a list of questions to ask. Make sure your questions are typed and convey the topics that are important to you in a company. Review your research and develop questions that will answer any questions that you have or were unable to uncover during your research. You should have five to ten detailed questions written out prior to the interview that will give you the best possible facts from which you will draw your final job decision.

Here are a few examples of questions you could ask the person with whom you meet:

- What do you know now about this industry that you didn't know before you entered it?

- Would you have done anything differently?

- What types of characteristics are important for success in this field or with your company?

- What makes XYZ Firm different from its competitors?

- What type of special education/certifications can I expect when working in this field?

When you are preparing for the interview, utilize the research you have already conducted. Read the company's annual report to gather pertinent information about the company's performance, products, locations, and so on. The purpose of the informational interview is to gather information about the company. However, the interviewer is also looking at your skills, knowledge, and dedication.

The next step of preparation is deciding what to wear. Your appearance for the informational interview is very important. (Refer to the "Dressing the Part" chapter within this book for clothing tips.)

The final step of preparation is your attitude. Remember, you are just gathering information and building your network.

Although you will be a little nervous, don't let the nerves get the best of you. You are not interviewing for a position; you are simply gathering data about a potential employer.

The key to a successful informational interview is first getting in the door. You have already accomplished that. Now you should focus on gathering information and showing the interviewer that you are a responsible and dedicated prospective employee who is diligently researching the opportunities for employment. You are already ahead of the game. Most job seekers are relying on their résumé to get them in the door. As a recruiter, I look for dedication and candidates who differentiate themselves among other job seekers. This technique of getting noticed is exactly that: a tool to differentiate you from John Doe job seeker.

During the interview, be yourself and smile. Remember that people are largely judged on appearance and attitude. Be personable, relax, and listen to every response. Make sure you ask specific questions. Also, make sure your questions are answered to your understanding. Remember that the interviewer is giving you his or her time and that you requested help. Be honest with the interviewer. He or she may turn out to be your best friend in the business.

Rules of the informational interview

Do not take a résumé with you. This may look like your informational interview is really a job interview and a way to get your foot in the door. Chances are, if your interview goes well, the interviewer will ask for your résumé. Tell the interviewer that you are still in the research stage of the job research process. Let them know that it was not your intent to present your résumé and that you sincerely appreciate his or her time and want to gather as much data as you can to make an educated decision. I recommend purchasing business cards that have your name, address, phone number, and e-mail address. Give the interviewer your card and ask if you can call in one week after your initial informational interviews. This step conveys that you are in demand and shows the interviewer that you are serious about your research.

Make sure you stick to your fifteen-minute appointment. Respect the interviewer's time. Be punctual. Arriving ten minutes before the scheduled appointment is sufficient.

Think of everyone you talk with or meet as a prospective employer. Following the actual informational interview, make sure you follow up appropriately. The same day, no later than the day after the interview, send a handwritten thank-you card to everyone you met with. If you told the interviewer you would call in one week, make sure you keep that promise. Following up and staying in touch with your network throughout your job search is very important.

In summary, the resources listed are effective tools that you can use to research and identify the companies and possible careers that best fit your goals and ambitions. These tools should narrow your potential target company list to only a few that match the criteria you desire and provide you with a validation of your career.

Chapter 3

Your Ticket to Success:
Your Résumé

*"The closest to perfection a person ever comes
is when he fills out a job application form."*
Stanley J. Randall

Your ticket to success is your résumé, which serves as a snapshot of your experiences, education, and activities. Your résumé is your ticket into the world of employment—most likely the first contact an employer has with you. How well it is constructed directly affects whether you are invited for an interview. This chapter illustrates a set of guidelines that lead to the development of a powerful résumé.

Design your résumé with a word processing program such as Microsoft Word™, which allows your résumé to be e-mailed and viewed by most word processing programs. I recommend using various style formats such as bold, underline, and italics to make your résumé attractive and pleasing to the eye. If you do not wish to write your own résumé, professional résumé services are available at various prices. Check the local Yellow Pages or Internet for a list of résumé service providers in your area. Although using a professional means some expense, you are usually assured of a top-quality job.

Whether you are typing your own résumé or using a service, be sure to have your résumé printed on high-quality paper. Good résumé paper is a thicker, textured paper usually made of at least some cotton, which conveys a high-quality image. Use color paper if possible because it stands out in a stack of résumés on a hiring manager's desk. Cream is a good color for women and light gray for men. Preparing your résumé to be distributed electronically is very important. Look at your résumé on your computer screen and scrutinize it as you would on paper. Does your résumé appear organized? Does it read well on the screen? Use a hyperlink for your e-mail address. Microsoft Word's default settings turn your e-mail address into a hyperlink for you. You may also want to consider more sophisticated programs such as Adobe Acrobat, which creates PDF files. While you may need to hire someone to create your résumé in this format, the result will be a very professional-looking document that will remain unchanged as it is e-mailed and posted electronically.

The most important requirements for your résumé are that it be neat and error-free. An error-free résumé illustrates attention to detail and pride in your work. Remember, competition for most positions is very strong, and the slightest error could cost you the opportunity to prove yourself worthy. Keep the font size between 10 point and 12 point. Smaller font sizes are difficult to read, and larger point sizes indicate to the employer that you are just trying to fill up space. Two people should edit your résumé for errors and clarity of wording.

Preparing a professional résumé is a multistage process. First, list all of your past accomplishments, responsibilities, or job positions on a piece of paper. Make this list as comprehensive as possible, because it will serve as a foundation for your résumé. Once you have the list, try to organize it in chronological order from present to past. Keep refining this list as you go forward with the rest of the résumé. Most people forget some of their accomplishments and responsibilities over time. This list helps you remember.

Should a résumé be one or two pages? That depends on the person and the content. If you have enough pertinent information (education, experience, and leadership skills that apply to the position) to fill up two full pages, then a two-page résumé is fine. If not, stick to a one-page résumé. Remember that the objective of sending a résumé is to obtain an interview. The résumé is not meant to contain a detailed description of every task you have completed at every job. The interview is the time to elaborate on all of your experiences. One page is fine if the information applies and offers a strong selling point for your skills.

Never have one and a half pages of résumé information. Use one full page or two full pages. That piece of advice notwithstanding, remember that the information on the résumé is important, not its length.

Identification

The first section of your résumé is the identification section: your contact information. At the top of your résumé, you should insert your complete name in large bold letters. The next step is to insert your complete address. Do not abbreviate anything. Fully spell out all words such as "street," "west," "Colorado," and so on. If you wish to identify both a college or temporary address and a permanent address, place them on opposite sides of the paper. Try to use only your current address or the address where the recruiters can find you today. Because your goal is to obtain an interview, they must be able to reach you.

Below your address, place your city, state, and zip code. Your telephone number(s), both daytime and evening, including your area code, go below the address information. Today's employers also expect an e-mail address. Make sure the address is professional. I do not recommend an e-mail address like cubsrock1234@yourISP.edu for a professional résumé. See Figure 2 for a sample of résumé header information.

Figure 2

Address Examples

Campus Address
Timothy J. Augustine
430 Lake Hall
Miami, Florida 44444
(555) 672-0000
Tim@yourISP.edu

Permanent Address
Timothy J. Augustine
2434 East White Street
Miami, Florida 44444
(555) 929-1111

If you have only one address, place it in the middle of the page:

Timothy J. Augustine
2434 East White Street
Miami, Florida 44444
(555) 929-1111
Tim@yourISP.edu

These examples can vary, but they are presented here as guidelines to follow. Remember that attention to detail could be the deciding factor. Don't let inattention to detail contribute to your competitor's success!

Objective or Summary

The next step is your career objective. An objective that describes your goals to the employer should be short and to the point, yet fully illustrate your desire and your professionalism. Remember that an employer has many résumés to review, and sometimes all they look at is your objective.

Most companies receive an average of two hundred to one thousand résumés for a given position. The slightest error or a poorly written general objective statement could send your résumé quickly to the circular file (the trash). Therefore, you need to make your objective statement eye-catching and to the point. Employers like to see objective statements that illustrate what you want to do for the company, not what you want the company to do for you. The objective reveals what you want to do, and the rest of the résumé develops the reasons that qualify you to do it.

You may also use a summary in place of an objective statement. A summary is often preferable when the applicant has significant work experience. A summary statement uses three to five strong sentences that highlight your accomplishments and link them to your career goals. You can highlight leadership skills, expertise, or personal strengths. Use either an objective or a summary, never both. Figure 3 illustrates examples of objective and summary statements.

Figure 3

Objective Examples

OBJECTIVE
> To obtain a position in medical supply sales that will give me the opportunity to use my medical background and communication skills to contribute to the success of the firm.

OBJECTIVE
> To obtain an entry-level position in accounting with a global financial services firm.

OBJECTIVE
> To obtain a challenging position that requires creativity and communication skills in the field of marketing.

Summary Examples

SUMMARY
> Bachelor's degree and an MBA degree in marketing from Northwestern University. Excellent presentation

and communication skills. Speak Italian and German. Experienced in all aspects of international marketing research.

SUMMARY

Bachelor's degree in financial management. Successfully completed an internship with XYZ Corporation in Cleveland, Ohio. Developed communication skills through Toastmasters International. President of student government and professional business fraternity.

SUMMARY

Global marketing executive with strong leadership experience in technology marketing, including company and product positioning, market segmentation definition, and analyst relations. Solid business foundation and experience in software sales and business development. Executive-level organizational leadership with well-rounded communication, presentation, teamwork, and interpersonal skills.

Again, these objectives and summaries are intended to offer a set of guidelines only. Many other ideas can also be very effective. Bounce ideas off other people during the editing process to create a résumé that best reflects your talents and strengths.

Education

The next step is your education. If you are currently a college student or a recent graduate, you should list your education after the objective statement. However, if you have more than five years of work experience, you should consider listing your professional work experience after your objective or summary statement. If you have relevant work experience, make sure it stands out on your résumé. The education should then follow.

For the education section, follow two steps. First, list your college education and then high school. The high school information, which can be left out to save room for other accomplishments, is really only needed if applicable in some way. If you have attended college, the company will assume that you graduated high school. However, if you do include high school information, you'll want to list your high school name, followed by the month and year of graduation. Include in this location your class rank, grade point average (GPA), class honors, and any other significant accomplishments.

In the education section, list your most recent degree first, followed by the month and year of graduation. Also list your college and its location. Illustrate your majors/minors and your GPA if it is greater than 3.0. If your GPA is lower than 3.0, you may not want to put it in writing. If it is not in writing, the interviewer may forget to ask. The final guideline to this section is your significant course work. List the classes you have excelled in and those that are pertinent to your major. However, try not to list more than four courses.

If you have significant work experience, place the education section after your work experience. Employers hire because of experience, but if you do not have a lot of experience, list education first (see Figure 4).

Figure 4

Education Examples

EDUCATION
>Bachelor of Business Administration: May 1994
>Ohio State University, Columbus, Ohio
>Major: Accounting
>GPA: 3.5
>
>High School:
>Lane Tech High School, Chicago, IL
>Valedictorian
>Diploma, May 1990

EDUCATION
   Bachelor of Business Administration: December 1996
   Columbia University, New York, NY
   Major: Marketing
   GPA: 4.0

EDUCATION
   Master of Business Administration: May 1996
   Wharton School of Business, Philadelphia, PA
   Concentration: Finance
   GPA: 3.6

   Bachelor of Business Administration, June 1990
   Duke University, Durham, NC
   Major: Finance
   GPA: 4.0

Work Experience

The next section is work experience. Any of a myriad of titles can head this section: Related Work Experience, Business Experience, Professional Experience, Internship, or Other Experience. Begin with your most recent experience. The first step is to list the company with a brief description, the title of the position you held and the dates in which you held the position. You should also include the employer's location (see Figure 5).

Figure 5

Work Experience Examples

ABC Software, Chicago, Illinois   **1994–Present**
   International software company with operations in the United States, Europe, South America, and Asia, targeting industries including financial services, telecommunications, insurance, and retail.

Vice President of Global Marketing   1999–Present

Senior-level business executive reporting directly to the chief executive officer. Held responsibility for worldwide market development activities, including category creation, company and product positioning, target market development, and revenue generation for new and existing software products and services.

- Developed a world-class marketing organization recognized by industry analysts.

- Held responsibility for the design and implementation of the market development plan, which focused on company positioning, brand development, market research, market analysis, and product launch.

Marketing Specialist   1994–1999

Member of a five-person global marketing team that was responsible for implementing various marketing programs such as event planning, marketing communications, market research, and Web design.

- Championed multiple customer and prospect industry forums, raised awareness of our company and products within our target markets of financial services, insurance, telecommunications, and retail.

- Developed and cultivated a customer advisory board that provided executive-level advice and direction regarding industry-specific solution development and customer relationship strategies.

As you describe your experience and responsibilities, try to use phrases rather than entire sentences and eliminate all personal pronouns such as "I," "me," and "my." You should use strong action words such as "achieved," "coordinated," and "designed" to describe what you accomplished. Describe how well you did the job and explain your accomplishments during the experience. As you describe your experiences, focus on the tasks assigned, activities involved in completing the tasks, and the quantifiable results (see Figure 6),

Another suggestion is to use nouns specifically related to your field. Employers often look for such buzzwords. For instance, include specific products, services, or programs with which you are familiar. One example would be, "Conducted order entry of stocks, bonds, and mutual funds." Upon scanning this résumé, the employer immediately notices that you are familiar with specific products used in that industry. Another suggestion is to include various programs or services you have used in school or previous jobs that might be applicable to an industry. For instance, you might indicate that you have conducted research using Dun and Bradstreet or Value Line.

This section of your résumé is very important, and you should spend significant time getting it right. Be creative in your descriptions. Take everyday tasks and turn them into traits useful to the employer. For instance, avoid general job descriptions such as "clerical work," "filing," or "answering phones." Instead, depict these tasks as "office management, information organization and retrieval, and customer service operations." Take each task you performed and illustrate how the experience has prepared you for other jobs. Be sure to use examples of experiences related to the job you want to obtain. In addition, try to quantify some of your information such as "increased revenue by 25 percent, reduced turnover by 10 percent, and managed a budget of $5.6M."

Too often, job seekers list every job they have had and what they did, just to have it written on the résumé. A better approach is to understand the skills required for the position you are applying for and to emphasize those traits. For instance, if you worked for four years as a waitress/waiter but had a one-semester internship in the field of your choice, elaborate on the internship and be brief with the food service job description. This presentation emphasizes the experience that is directly related to your career goals, and downplays jobs you have taken just for the money. However, a waitress/waiter job is not without value because success in that position demonstrates solid communication, social, and customer service skills.

The following list offers action words you could use.

accomplished	achieved
acquired	administered
advised	appointed
assessed	assisted
assured	brought
budgeted	championed
collaborated	communicated
composed	controlled
coordinated	delegated
demonstrated	developed
educated	encouraged
established	evaluated
expedited	formulated
fostered	implemented
initiated	led
maintained	motivated
negotiated	organized
persuaded	programmed
recommended	researched
reviewed	selected
strengthened	supervised
supported	targeted
transformed	tutored
worked	

Figure 6

Work and Related Experience Examples

RELATED EXPERIENCE
Sales Executive   **1999–2003**

Held responsibility for business development and large-account management, selling software products and services within a geographic region. Focused sales activity within the financial services, telecommunications, and retail industries.

- Managed a comprehensive sales cycle, which consisted of prospecting, needs analysis, proof of concept, proposal, billing, and collection with an average cycle time of six to nine months.

- Exceeded personal sales quota by 25 percent annually.

WORK EXPERIENCE
Account Executive Midwest Region   **2000–Present**

- Held responsibility for account management and strategic customer partnerships with Hamburgerland's corporate and franchise stores as well as independent and national food distributors.

- Managed multiple sales cycles and product rollouts within Ohio, Michigan, Indiana, Pennsylvania, and Illinois.

OTHER WORK EXPERIENCE
Brand Manager, XYZ Cheese   **1999–2002**

- Held responsibility for all promotions, trade support, financial tracking, competitive analysis, and new product development to including positioning, product development, packaging, pricing, marketing plan, and management of sell-in.

- Managed the XYZ Cheese business, including a $19 million advertising and promotion budget. Brand delivered volume, share, and record profit growth, reversing historical declines.

- Led breakthrough product introductions that grew grated cheese volume by 12 percent.

Computer Tutor, University of Michigan   Summer, 1999

- Developed training classes for computer methods.

- Instructed classes of 15–20 students, focusing on Microsoft products.

- Served as a computer engineer for the computer lab and completed tasks including updating existing systems and converting to a new platform.

The work experience section of a résumé reveals to the employer what you can do as well as what you have accomplished. Make each point stand out in order to reveal your hard work and to also illustrate your devotion to past jobs. Consistency is the important key in this section. If you use boldface type for your position in one instance, use it for your position every time. Notice the dates in the examples. They can either be in months or years. I prefer years because this might visually give you a full year of more work experience. During the interview you will discuss the exact timing of past jobs, but this approach might propel you past the front door or past the gatekeeper reviewing the résumés. Remember to be honest, professional, and creative, and most importantly, pay attention to detail!

Leadership

The next section of the résumé illustrates leadership experience and extracurricular activities, both of which show energy, initiative, and interpersonal skills. In this section you also want to use past-tense action words. Your goal is to show how well you performed during these experiences.

First, list the position(s) held and state the name of the organization. Also include the location of the organization and indicate the time span of the position. Figure 7 gives leadership examples.

Figure 7

Leadership Section for a Résumé

LEADERSHIP SKILLS
Board of Directors,
Naperville Career Center   **2002–2003**
     Acted on behalf of the career center with organizational funding and scheduling of activities, as well as evaluating and implementing services provided to the community.

President, XYZ
Leadership Board, XYZ University   **1999–2001**
     Planned monthly meetings and secured professional speakers.
     Followed Robert's Rules of Order and functioned as liaison between student body and faculty.

Vice President,
Ski Club, Chicago, Illinois   **1998–2000**
     Assisted the president with management of this eighty-member club.
     Planned trips to Denver, and instructed new members on different techniques of skiing.

President, Delta Sigma Pi,
Polytechnic University   **2001–2002**
     Professional business fraternity.

Formulated the structure for the 108-member Polytechnic chapter and all of its activities.

Honors

After describing your leadership roles, follow with the honors section. List the activities in which you have received honors. List your high school activities or honors only if they are significant or applicable and only if high school education was included in your Education section. Examples of honors are found in Figure 8.

Figure 8

Honors Section for a Résumé

HONORS

College	**High School**
Dean's list, eight semesters	Valedictorian
National Dean's List, 2000	
Honor roll, Delta Sigma Pi, 2000	
Golden Key Award, 2000	
Delegate of Kent State, Beta Pi Chapter, Delta Sigma Pi, 2000	

Hobbies/Interests

If you have space available and the material relates to your job search, the next section of the résumé may be devoted to your hobbies and interests. This section shows the employer you are a well-rounded individual. You may want to outline your travel experience, hobbies, and special interests. Depending on the job and the company, you may want to consider not placing this section on your résumé. Examples can be found in Figure 9.

Figure 9

Hobbies and Interests Section for a Résumé

INTERESTS
Golf, reading, theater, and international travel.

PERSONAL INTERESTS
Camping, spectator sports, golf, boating, and fishing.

The purpose of illustrating your hobbies is to establish common ground with the employer. Do not try to make up hobbies. The interviewer may ask you about the hobbies, and you would have no intelligent idea what to say. Remember to always be honest. Your reputation stays with you.

References

The final section is for references. It usually states that character references can be provided if necessary. This section is now considered optional. Employers often assume that references are available upon request. Therefore, you may choose to omit this section if you wish to conserve space. On the other hand, you may want to include the actual list of references with your résumé. In this case, you would simply list each reference's name, title, company, address, and phone number on an additional page to include with your résumé. If you do include references, have four to six names listed. Examples of such references appear in Figure 10.

Figure 10

Reference Section for a Résumé

REFERENCES
Available upon request

(On a separate page)

REFERENCES

Joe Smith
Vice President of Manufacturing
Rotomola Corporation
123 Main Street
Chicago, IL 99999
(555) 456-7890

During your interview, you should always be prepared to present your references. Have at least six references identified. You should include two professional references from people you have worked with in the past. You should have two peer references that include friends who could serve as a character reference. Finally, have two reference letters from either a professor or a manager. Make sure you contact the references prior to providing their names to the recruiter. Call your intended references and ask for their permission to offer their names. Tell them about the position you are considering. You should also let them know the expected timeframe of the call, if your potential employer does in fact check your references.

Developing Your Cover Letter

When mailing your résumé, you need to enclose a cover letter, a simple document designed to give an overview of your objectives, qualifications, and most importantly the value that you can bring to the company or organization. As you develop this letter, you need to answer three questions:

- "What problems does the potential employer have that need to be solved?"

- "How can I highlight my strengths, and show in this introduction letter that I can help the employer?"

- "How can I show the value that I can bring to the organization?"

The letter should be addressed to a specific person. Find out the name and title of the human resource director or the hiring manager rather than addressing the letter to "Dear Sir or Madam." The letter should be three to four paragraphs long and convey the value that you can provide as well as your interest in a specific position with the prospective firm. In addition, the letters should be focused on the employers' needs instead of your wants. Your focus on the employer, rather than on yourself, always earns more attention, interest, and action.

The cover letter is segmented into three parts:

Introduction

The introduction is typically a statement that mentions the position you are interested in and how you learned about it. Keep in mind that the recruiter or hiring manager reads many of these documents, so keep the introduction interesting and relevant.

> Example: "I am writing in response to an open sales manager position for the Chicago region. I learned of this opportunity through the Sales and Marketing Executives of Chicago, where I serve on the Board of Directors. Throughout my professional career, I have prided myself in continually proving my ability to build customer relationships, coach sales teams, and grow revenues."

Body

The body of the cover letter is typically a one- or two-paragraph summary of your skills, knowledge, experience, and career goals. Focus this section on your understanding of the employer's needs, and match your strengths to those needs.

> Example: "Based on my knowledge of XYZ

Company, I feel that the product line is competitive, the organizational reputation is strong, and the customer base is solid. The candidate you are looking for should be well versed in consultative selling and large account management, as well as provide a solid level of technical understanding needed to lead a sales team. As you can see from my enclosed résumé, I have successfully performed at ABC Software for eight years, growing the business by 45 percent annually. Prior to joining ABC Software, I worked for X Software for twelve years, growing sales revenue annually and exceeding my quota of $2 million in sales of products and services per year. Through this work experience, I feel that I can quickly transfer my skills to help XYZ Company hit their regional goals of $5 million as stated in your annual report."

Conclusion

The final paragraph highlights the action that you want the employer to take. You also introduce your qualifications in this section and request a phone call to set up an interview if interested. Make sure your final paragraph is confident and that it suggests a meeting or invites the recruiter to take further action.

Example: "Given my skills in relationship selling, familiarity with the product line, and understanding of your clients' needs, I believe I could be of immediate value to XYZ Company. I would welcome the opportunity to meet with you to review my qualifications and to better understand your needs for the position."

Figures 11–13 show examples of résumés and cover letters that apply the guidelines mentioned in this chapter. Analyze each of them. Take different ideas from them and build your own perfect résumé and cover letter to best represent you to prospective employees.

Figure 11

Entry-Level Résumé Example

JANE DOE
1000 Oak Lane
Columbus, Ohio 44240
(555) 777-1000
janedoe@yourISP.edu

Objective:	To obtain a human resources training position with an organization that affords me the opportunity to contribute through my knowledge and training experience.
Education:	Ohio State University, Columbus, Ohio Bachelor of Business Administration: May 2003 Major: Human Resource Management GPA 3.5
Experience:	*Internship, Columbus Direct Financial Software,* *Columbus, Ohio 2003–2004* Held responsibility for business development within the finance industry. Secured 15 new customers, including National City, Huntington Bank, and PNC Bank. *Server/Trainer, Mario's,* *Cuyahoga Falls, Ohio 2001–2003* Established training programs for new employees resulting in 25 percent productivity increase. Maintained daily cash flows of $2,000. Held responsibility for enthusiastic quality service. *Data Entry Specialist, King Office Products,* *New Philadelphia, Ohio 1999–2001*

Held responsibility for inventory control merchandise levels for daily operation.
Conducted sales training programs based on SPIN Selling Program.

Customer Service Representative, Andy's Shoes,
New Philadelphia, Ohio 1997–1999

Developed promotional programs resulting in a 45 percent annual increase in sales.
Managed monthly training programs for 25 associates focused on product knowledge.

Professional
Organizations: Society for Human Resource Management (SHRM) 1999–Present

Recognition Director
Formulated recognition programs for students' professional development in other organizations during their college career.

Director of Administration
Devised administrative data documenting student activities.

External Affairs Chair
Maintained correspondence with alumni and other chapters. Acted as a liaison between the local SHRM chapter and the OSU College of Business.

Delta Sigma Pi, Professional Business Fraternity 2000–Present

President
Formulated the structure for the 108-member chapter and all of its activities.

Honors/
Awards: Golden Rose Society Award
Ohio State University Outstanding Service Award
Ohio State University Orientation Micro Teacher Award
Ohio State University Homecoming Court Nominee

References: Available upon request

Figure 12

Mid-Level Résumé Example

John Smith

430 Main Street • Pleasanton, California 65588 • 555-255-4227 • jsmith@yourISP.edu

SUMMARY

Experienced leader with an MBA and excellent project management, problem solving, analytical, and communication skills. Solid background in Fortune 100 telecommunications consulting and insurance marketing, product development, and operations. Proven success working in both team and independent environments.

PROFESSIONAL EXPERIENCE

XYZ Corp., Chicago, IL   *2000–Present*

A management consulting and technology services organization with more than $11 billion in annual revenue.

Consultant, Communications and High-Tech Market, 2001–2002

Supervised teams of consultant and client personnel, created work plans, managed the timely completion of project deliverables, built and maintained strong client relationships, facilitated group discussions, reported team status to project senior management, documented system requirements, and mentored junior project members.

- Team Lead, CRM Project: Identified business and technical requirements, selected an contract management software solution, and implemented this software for more than 25,000 customer service representatives. This initiative was part of a multiyear CRM program to transition a Fortune 100 telecommunications firm from a product to a customer focus.
- Created the User Acceptance Test (UAT) work plan, schedule, approach document, and scenario template.
- Coordinated (UAT) project test schedules and entry/exit criteria with the leaders of all other test teams.
- Supervised and directed the work of consultant and client personnel to collect technical requirements.
- Documented call center volume data and infrastructure cost information for the contract management software selection.
- Developed an inventory of the data elements to be used by the contract management software.
- Created statement of work documents to describe the function, data flow, and requirements of several incumbent computer systems that the contract management software would interface

Business Analyst, Central Office Project, 2001
- Evaluated client needs to design and implement a software application to manage technician workflow, work assignment, and time reporting. This application resided on a wireless handheld device, presented a standardized user interface, and connected with the necessary legacy systems.
- Analyzed and assessed high-level project goals to produce business vision and project assessment documents.
- Created process flow and system documentation through site visits and subject-matter expert interviews.
- Co-led a requirements preparation team to create process templates.

Team Lead, Technician of the Future Project (CIO magazine CIO-100 award winner, August 2001)
- Project team developed an enterprise-wide application for more than 30,000 field technicians of a Fortune 100 telecommunications firm to be used for job dispatch, trouble testing, material ordering, and time reporting. This application interfaced with numerous legacy systems, presented a single standardized platform, and was deployed on a durable laptop that used wireless technology.
- Trained and managed a team of consultant and client personnel to provide test data support to all project teams including development, product test, QA test, architecture, and infrastructure.
- Implemented several process improvements for system flow-through and test data in faster detection and correction of system defects.
- Ensured on-time delivery of the application by coordinating issue resolution through communication with other teams and client organizations.

Analyst, Communications and High-Tech Market, 2000–2001
- Developed problem-solving skills, gained knowledge of the telecommunications industry, ensured timely completion of project deliverables, reported status to team leadership, built and maintained strong client relationships, and produced process improvements.
- Championed the project team's knowledge building and test data coordination for the application's most critical and widely used legacy system.
- Developed contacts with client personnel, and leveraged relationships to solve complex issues.

XYZ Insurance Company, Livermore, AR, 1991–2000
A life and health insurance company with 300 employees and $188 million in assets.

Manager, Life Marketing, 1997–2000
- Managed the operational, product development, training, and administrative functions for the life line of business. Created and implemented plans to promote and protect profitability.
- Led a team during a nine-month project that developed an on-site, NASD-licensed broker-dealer branch office.

- Managed a 10-month project team that outsourced the premium billing, remittance, and broker-dealer functions to a third party administrator. This protected approximately $4 million in annualized premium.
- Solved problems and gave direction as the point person for approximately 40 people across departments including customer service, marketing, new underwriting, programming, accounting, and agent licensing.

Account Coordinator, Life Marketing, 1994–1997
- Served as a liaison between lead marketers, a sales force of over 1,500 agents, and all home office departments. Reduced costs and improved customer service through process improvements to internal systems.
- Created and implemented a product promotion financing system with annual value of $675,000.
- Led a project team that analyzed and revised a management/agent/product information system. This 8-month project resulted in the production of a reliable field management reporting system.
- Analyzed and streamlined the new business and underwriting workflow process that reduced turnaround time by 30 percent and significantly increased agent retention and acquisition.
- Designed and implemented programs to monitor agent financial activity, which improved agent debt collection and control.

Supervisor, Commission Accounting, 1993–1994
- Ensured timely and accurate payment of commissions to 200 agents weekly and 5,000 agents monthly. Resolved issues through communication and teamwork with other departments. Trained and supervised a staff of three.
- Created and implemented a system that generated and monitored financial loans to agents.

Management Trainee/Internal Auditor, 1991–1993
- Performed departmental rotations through all administrative and sales support areas.
- Recovered more than $100,000 in erroneously paid agent commissions through monthly audits.

EDUCATION
- Blue Wave University, Festus, MO, Master of Business Administration (Management & Finance): 1999
- Member of Beta Gamma Sigma Honor Society: 1999
- University of Alabama, Tuscaloosa, AL, Bachelor of Arts in Economics: 1991
- Alabama Economic Society: 1991
- Fellow, Life Management Institute (FLMI): 1994

Figure 13

Senior-Level Résumé Example

Bill Johnson
1234 White Street
Naperville, Illinois 99999
555-505-1000
Bjohnson@yourISP.edu

SUMMARY

Senior information technology executive, with a strong background in insurance, financial services, and technology. Significant experience in general management, organizational transformation, systems management, reengineering, project management, application development and delivery, leadership development, team building, and expense management.

PROFESSIONAL EXPERIENCE

XYZ INSURANCE COMPANY, Maplegrove, MS 1968–Present
The nation's largest publicly held personal lines insurer, XYZ provides insurance products to more than 14 million households and has approximately 13,000 exclusive agents in the U.S. and Canada.

Assistant Vice President, Marketing and Data Services 2000–Present
- Managed a $74 million IT organization responsible for developing and supporting XYZ's corporate marketing processes including Customer Relationship (CRM), Data Warehousing, Document Management, Internet and Office Technologies, Customer Documents, and Billing.
- Created and led the Systems organization that supports the corporate and personal lines marketing processes, which resulted in the early delivery of several major CRM infrastructure components including campaign management, data mart, and desktop tools, a predictive modeling environment, and message brokering capabilities.
- Managed I/T expenses to support marketing functions, resulting in a favorable 2001 year-end expense variance of $1.5 million (or 2 percent) on a budget of $74.2 million.

Assistant Vice President, Enterprise Technologies 1998–2000
- Managed a $76 million Systems organization responsible for supporting XYZ's corporate financial, statistical, human resources, and professional office processes.
- Managed the I/T expenses for the support of the back office and administrative functions, while continuing to upgrade XYZ's overall technology infrastructure. Delivered a favorable variance of

$4.4 million (or 4.9 percent) on a 1999 budget of $89.5 million as well as a favorable variance of $4.7 million (or 6.1 percent) on a budget of $76.8 million in 2000.

- Created, funded, and directed a high-performance team that developed and implemented a client household database that enabled XYZ to interact seamlessly with customers via the Internet, a call center, or an agent.
- Created a high-performance team that developed a Comparative Rater application to analyze the competitive automobile pricing environment within five target market states. Pilot was delivered in 120 days and within budget.

Assistant Vice President, Application Architecture and Strategies 1995–1998

Managed a highly technical organization that established and maintained XYZ's systems architecture, architecture that set the company's strategic technology direction.

- Created, funded, and directed a Document Management initiative that developed and implemented a robust document archive and image infrastructure which resulted in fewer redundancies and overall cost reductions of several million dollars.
- Created, funded, and led a $20+ million Enterprise Data Warehousing initiative that developed and implemented a series of disciplined data management processes and a robust data warehousing infrastructure resulting in overall cost reductions of several million dollars.
- Created, funded, and directed a new communication team, resulting in more effective management of internal technology communications and external media releases.

Assistant Vice President, Reinvention Team 1994–1995

Participated on a senior-level business reengineering team commissioned by the chairman, CEO, and senior management team.

- Created and led an Enterprise Architect team that established and maintained technology standards, resulting in a more highly disciplined I/T development process with more effective use of technology resources.
- Created and led the development of the first enterprise Information Technology Strategic Plan, which provided a detailed roadmap for the major I/T initiatives that would be required to support the anticipated growth of the company into the new millennium. Plan resulted in a highly disciplined, multiyear investment of more than $1 billion with fewer redundancies and lower overall infrastructure costs.
- Provided technology and organizational design consultation to senior management team that successfully reengineered several major cus-

tomer relationship processes, resulting in improved customer satisfaction and product development cycle time and lower overall expenses.

Assistant Vice President, Commercial Insurance Systems 1968–1994
Managed a $35 million Systems organization and data center, which supported the commercial insurance applications for three profit centers.

- Led the successful transformation of an internally focused Systems department into a client-focused I/T Consulting organization that was instrumental in the overall turnaround of the Commercial Insurance Division, resulting in reduced I/T expenses, increased productivity, and a dramatic improvement in client satisfaction.
- Created and led a senior management governance team and resource allocation process for prioritizing and funding major I/T initiatives, resulting in an overall reduction in expenses and more effective allocation of technology resources.

EDUCATION

Northsouthern University, Columbia, TN
Master of Business Administration, Accounting and Information Systems: 1994

Red Clover University, Boulder Junction, WI
Bachelor of Arts, Economics and Sociology: 1968

MEMBERSHIPS AND AFFILIATIONS

Colleges and Universities 1996–Present
Officer sponsor of XYZ's Northsouthern University recruiting team

Society for Information Management (SIM) 1996–Present
- Member of Naperville Chapter
- Member of SIM International Executive Board—VP of Enterprise Programs

Life Office Management Association (LOMA) 1998–2001
XYZ's representative to Property and Casualty Systems Committee

Insurance Accounting and Systems Association (IASA) 1985–1990
Member, chaired systems research and program committees

National Association of Independent Insurers (NAII) 1985–1990
Member, chaired program committee

PROFESSIONAL REFERENCES
Available upon request

Figure 14

Cover Letter Examples

Jane Doe
555 East Third Street
Jacksonville, Florida 22222
(555) 567-0000

April 17, 2003

Mr. John Smith
Director, Florida State Social Services
600 Water Street
Jacksonville, Florida 22222

Dear Mr. Smith:

In June 2003, I will receive my Bachelor of Arts degree from Florida State University, pending the completion of my foreign language requirement. I am writing to express my interest in obtaining a position with your agency.

As you will see from the enclosed résumé, I majored in psychology and criminal justice, and achieved a 3.0 and 3.2 GPA, respectively. For the past one and a half years, I have been employed as a case manager for the Florida Temporary Homeless Shelter, and volunteered at the same agency for six months prior to my present employment. This experience has afforded me the opportunity to learn the functions of a homeless shelter and allowed me to participate in decisions regarding updating shelter policies and documentation procedures.

Realizing that this summary, as well as my résumé, cannot adequately communicate my qualifications in depth, I would appreciate the opportunity to discuss with you in person how I might become an asset to your agency.

Sincerely,

Jane Doe

Enclosure

Julie Smith
123 North Meadows Street
Springfield, Ohio 55555
(555) 333-4444

September 1, 2003

Ms. Margaret Evans
Regional Director of Human Resources
XYZ Corporation
Naperville, Illinois 33333

Dear Ms. Evans:

I am writing in reference to the advertised employment opportunity in the marketing department at XYZ. I will finish my coursework toward a bachelor's of business administration and will receive my degree in December of this year. Please accept my résumé and letter for your review.

My business experience and educational endeavors have prepared me for a career in the field of marketing. I have worked as a sales representative for several years, which has captured my interests. In addition, I have had success in my course work and shall be graduating with honors.

The enclosed résumé highlights several other achievements, experiences, and awards. I have also had extensive involvement in work, classes, and various organizations in which I had opportunities to perform individually and as part of a team. Further, I have strengthened my skills in human relations, communications, and leadership through my co-curricular activities.

I would welcome an opportunity to meet with you to discuss my qualifications. Please contact me at (555) 333-4444. I may also be contacted via the Internet at jsmith@yourISP.edu.

Sincerely,

Julie Smith

Enclosure

James Jackson
123 Wilson Drive
Phoenix, Arizona 11111
(555) 222-9999

September 5, 2003

Mr. Edward Smiles
XYZ Corporation
Rochester, New York 88888

Dear Mr. Smiles:

I am very interested in obtaining a position with your organization where I can apply my educational background in technology to the field of telecommunications.

While attending the University of Colorado, I gained hands-on training for the latest technological advancements in the telecommunications field. In addition, as President of the American Marketing Association at UC, I designed new marketing efforts, which effectively increased membership over 30 percent in just one year. Further, as a student senator, I was part of crafting vision and mission statements for the student body.

I will be receiving a bachelor's degree in marketing and communications in December of this year and am currently searching for employment opportunities. Enclosed is my résumé and list of references. I believe I would make an immediate and positive contribution to your firm. In addition, I am interested in the prospect of relocation to the New York area.

I would welcome an opportunity to discuss the possibility of employment with your firm. Please contact me at (555) 222-9999.

Sincerely,

James Jackson

Enclosure

Chapter 4

Dressing the Part

You have probably heard the saying, "You never get a second chance to make a first impression." But did you know that about 85 percent of what you convey during this first impression is through nonverbal communication? My research shows almost 85 percent of what is communicated in any situation is nonverbal. Therefore, your dress and visual presence can have a profound effect on your chances of obtaining the position you desire.

The basic premise of this section is that perception is everything. How the company views you, how you view yourself, and how you want others to view you all play a role in the "game" of interviewing. The manner in which you conduct yourself is just as important as what you say.

Basic Rules
Dress appropriately for the industry.
Conservative firms—such as in the financial, insurance, and accounting industries—require a very professional appearance. However, a relaxed or creative industry—marketing, advertising, and journalism—may be more impressed with a little more individualistic style. Regardless of the situation, flamboyance is not a wise choice! You want to be remembered

for what you say, what you have done, and what you can offer
to the company.

Dress in a manner that conforms to the specific company or organization.

Take a look around the office during your informational
interview. Look at how the employees are dressed. You should
strive to dress equally with the managers who might be conducting the interview.

When in doubt, dress up, not down.

It is always better to be more professionally dressed rather
than less. While many firms today allow casual dress on a daily
basis, the interviewee should be professionally dressed.

Personal hygiene is a necessity.

Be sure your hair is neat and clean. Make sure your fin-
gernails are clean and trim. Check for stains or wrinkles in
your clothing. Avoid excessive cologne. Take a look into the
mirror before you leave for the interview to conduct one last
check of your appearance. Finally, make sure you brush your
teeth or take breath mints with you!

Avoid distractions.

Preferably avoid wearing anything that identifies any beliefs or personal associations, such as religious beliefs or political affiliation. In addition, avoid wearing any items that are
considered masculine for a woman or feminine for a man (for
example, a necktie for a woman or an earring on a man).
These items are often distractions and could take the interviewer's attention away from what you have to say.

For Women

The most important thing to consider when choosing the
clothing for an interview is the fit. Uncomfortable clothing

will make an already uncomfortable situation worse. You have more important things to worry about than your suit being too small, shoes being too tight, or blouse sleeves being too short. If you plan to shop for an interview suit, be sure to do it a couple of weeks ahead of time. Then you can choose the best-fitting clothing without having to scramble at the last minute for something to wear. Shopping early also gives you the opportunity to shop for matching accessories.

The best attire for interviews is a suit. A basic blazer and matching skirt are preferred. Slacks are also considered professional attire for the interview stage. A dress may be worn, but is not recommended for the first interview. If a dress is worn, it should be a professional-looking dress, preferably with a blazer.

When wearing a suit, the blazer should be fairly conservative. Extra wide collars or other trendy designs have no positive impact in an interview. A double-breasted suit tends to look more professional, whereas the single is more casual; either is acceptable. Try to avoid big bright buttons or other distracting items attached to the blazer; these only divert the interviewer's attention. The skirt should be right around knee length, or perhaps one to two inches above. Shorter lengths are not recommended.

The type of material can make or break the suit. Wool is the preferred material, but consider the climate and season. A lighter weight material such as linen or quality blends may be sufficient. I stress the word "quality." You should wear clothing that looks as if it is of high quality.

When in doubt, wear navy blue. Although other colors may suffice, navy blue is still considered classic. Again, depending on the perception you want to instill and the type of company you are interviewing with, other colors may be worn. Shades of gray are also considered conservative. Certainly, some sort of dark-colored suit is preferred for the first interview. The second interview may allow for more freedom in color choice, such as dark green, red, or brown. During the

second interview, you may also wear a classic dress with a
jacket. A small print in the fabric is also acceptable as long as
it does not divert the attention of the interviewer. Pastels are
generally not good interviewing suit colors.

Your suit should be neat, pressed, and free of lint, which
displays to the interviewer a pride in appearance. The time you
took to prepare for the interview is taken into consideration. If
your suit is wrinkled, you appear as if you did not plan ahead
for the interview and do not care about getting the job.

Generally, a blouse or shell should be worn underneath
the blazer. Absolutely never wear camisoles. They do not convey the right impression in an interview. The blouse should
not be transparent and should not be cut too low in the front.
The blouse should be crisp and clean. A white blouse does a
good job of giving a bright, clean look. Cream and ivory are
also acceptable colors. Finally, the blouse should not be too
frilly or have too large of a bow or other designs, as these
cause distractions.

Proper accessories can help make a great first impression.
Choose nylons to match the bottom of your skirt. For instance,
if the bottom of the skirt is black, wear black nylons; if navy,
wear navy ones. If matching the skirt is not possible, wear nude
nylons or taupe. The idea is to create one solid flow from head
to toe with no distractions. If you have a white blouse, black
skirt, and white nylons, there is a distraction in the flow. When
in doubt, go for the nude-colored nylons.

Shoes are an equally important part of the attire. Many
people do not realize that shoes are very noticeable items, especially if they do not conform to the rest of the outfit. Make
sure they look professional and are shined. They should be sen-
sible and not too flashy. Try to avoid decorative designs or
fancy bows. They should be slip on, rather than with some sort
of tying or buckling required. Proper fit should also be considered as you may be wearing them for a long time. Pumps are
good interviewing shoes for women. A small to medium half-
inch to two-inch heel is suggested for all women, regardless of

height. Your shoes should also match the bottom of your skirt, which continues the visual flow without distractions.

A small amount of jewelry may enhance your appearance. However, the idea is to keep it simple. The best bet would be to wear just earrings and a watch. A nice dress watch is certainly acceptable and can come in handy to avoid being late. Avoid plastic, large-faced watches. A simple gold, silver, or even conservative leather-strapped watch is appropriate. Earrings are great accessories that seem to set off the face in a positive way. The best ones are small to medium in size and cover the lower one-quarter to one-third part of the earlobe. It is preferable to wear either gold or silver. Wear only one earring per ear; do not wear dangling earrings.

Other jewelry may be worn, but should be kept to a minimum. Rings are acceptable, but try to limit them to one or two per hand. Conservative bracelets are acceptable, but should be kept to a minimum and should not include bangle bracelets (they tend to clank and make noise). A necklace may be worn as well. However, only wear one necklace and avoid large pendants. Small to medium-sized pins on a lapel are attractive and professional, but remember to stay simple. The best rule of thumb is to prevent distracting attention with your jewelry. Remember, you want the interviewer to remember you, not the earrings or bracelets you wore.

Finally, women should be careful when applying cologne or perfume. It is actually a better idea to go without cologne for an interview. An allergic reaction by the interviewer could cause the interview to end quickly. If you want to wear cologne, better to apply just a small bit rather than to overdo it.

For Men

The basic interview attire for a man is a suit. Again, look to the industry and individual company to gain a perspective of how to dress. For a conservative company or industry, a single-breasted suit is recommended. A single-breasted suit is one in which the buttons and the jacket opening are vertical. With a double-breasted suit, the jacket that has overlapping fronts that give a double thickness of cloth. For a less conservative firm, I recommend a double-breasted suit. When in doubt, dress more conservatively and wear a single-breasted suit.

When selecting a suit, consider your body type. Short or stocky body types should avoid the double-breasted suit, which makes you appear heavier than you are. Ask for the help of experienced sales personnel in the men's department of your local department store or a men's shop where suits are sold. They often have the best advice for fitting your body type.

The suit material should be wool. High-quality blended suits are also acceptable but often do not last as long and do not lay on one's body correctly after repeated cleanings. Quality is key. You should put as much emphasis on your suit as your résumé. A high-quality suit shows attention to detail and pride in appearance.

The color of the suit should be neutral, usually navy or shades of gray. Stay away from pinstripe suits. These suits have traditionally been power suits and are usually worn by executives. You may appear to be a threat or perceived as a corporate climber if your clothing is too flashy.

Your tie should also be a neutral color. You want to offset the color of the suit, but you don't want to take the interviewer's attention away from you. With a navy blue suit, you could wear a blue or red tie with some type of design. Try to stay away from pastels or flashy loud designs. Usually the salesperson where you purchase your suit and tie knows what you are looking for and can recommend and match accordingly. Use your best judgment, and consult your friends about what looks good and what does not.

Your shirt is also an important part of the interviewing outfit. Again, it depends on the color of the suit. A white, 100 percent cotton shirt cleaned and pressed with light starch is always a good idea. Again, quality cotton/polyester shirts are also good, keeping quality in mind. You want to show the interviewer that you focus on quality in everything you do. With a single-breasted suit, a pointed collar shirt looks more professional. With a double-breasted suit, the button-down collar is more professional. Above all else, make sure the shirt fits well and allows room for flexibility.

The best shoes to wear for an interview are wingtips or nice loafers. Do not wear penny loafers, boots, or boat shoes, as these present a more trendy or casual look. The color of the shoes depends on your suit. The most common colors worn by professionals have been cordovan or black shoes. Along with your shoes, socks are very important. Make sure they match your suit and are also of high quality. Make sure your socks cover your calf muscle. You do not want to expose any leg skin when you cross your legs. Do not wear socks with holes in the toes or heels. What would happen if the interviewer asked you to take your shoes off to walk in his or her office? (Don't worry, this doesn't happen often, but it is best to be prepared.) You also want your belt to be in good condition without signs of wear. Make sure you did not miss any belt loops. If the interviewer asks you to remove your jacket, your belt will show.

For Both

Don't forget that the most important thing to wear is a smile. Keep a positive mental attitude. You have worked hard to get where you are and you owe it to yourself. Stand tall, but not stiffly. Show the interviewer you are ready and willing to help this company succeed.

In addition, remember a few other tips. Take a lint roller with you to take off any dog hair, lint, or dandruff. Make sure you take a damp washcloth in your car, which you can use to clean and shine your shoes one last time, giving the interviewer the impression of well-groomed shoes. Finally, do not forget to take items that are needed for elements such as snow and rain. Take an umbrella if it is raining. This little detail makes a big difference for an interview. If it is snowing, feel free to wear boots or galoshes to the interview and carry your dress shoes. Change in the lobby if needed. The last thing you want to think about during the interview is wet socks and pants because you had to walk through the snow. I understand that this discussion sounds very basic, but people often forget the smallest details.

Before you leave your house, make sure you cover all the basics. Your hair should be well groomed. I recommend using hair spray to keep it in place. If you have a trendy hairstyle, you might consider toning it down for the interview to match your conservative professional appearance.

When you look in the mirror, you must feel good about your appearance and not focus on it. During the interview you should be focused on what you want to say. Give the interviewer your best for his or her first impression. Take care of yourself and your appearance. Good luck and look your best!

Figure 15 summarizes the do's and don'ts of dressing the part.

Figure 15

Dressing the Part

WOMEN

	DO's	DON'Ts
Suit	Navy, gray, dark green, black, burgundy, dark brown	Purple, yellow, pastels
Blouse	Silk-like fabric	Camisoles
	Feminine/subtle design	Low cut
	White, cream, ivory	Pastels
Skirt	1–2" above the knee	Higher than 2" above knee
	1" below calf muscle	High slits
	Conservative slit up back or side	

Shoes	Pumps	High heels (above 2")
	0–2" heel	Uncomfortable fit
	Match to nylons or bottom of skirt	
Accessories	One earring per ear	Bangle bracelets
	Two rings maximum	Several necklaces
	Dress watch	Piercing (other than ear)
	Lapel pin	Political or religious pins
Nylons	Match to bottom of skirt	White colored
	Nude or tan colored	

MEN

	DO's	DON'Ts
Suit	Navy, black, shades of gray	Brown, pinstripe
	100 percent wool	Poor polyester blend
	Quality blends	
Shoes	Wingtips	Penny loafers
	Professional loafers	Tasseled shoes
Shirt	White, light blue	Large stripes
	Small stripe	Pastels or dark colors
	Pressed and clean	
Tie	Blue, red, yellow	Crazy/funny designs
	Subtle print	Loud stripes
Accessories	One ring at most	Earrings
	Dress watch	Bracelets
		Tie clips or collar bars
		Handkerchief in pocket

Chapter 5

The Spotlight: The Interview

The spotlight is the interview. You have done your preparation, identified target companies, started your company research, and have been asked to schedule an interview. In this chapter, you explore the types of interviews you might face, the topics that are most likely to be covered in the interview, and techniques to prepare before the interview. Once you are prepared, we explore the event of the interview, what to expect after the first interview, and how to deal with rejection, acceptance, and salary negotiation.

First, you need to understand the different types of interviews you may face during your job search. The four most common types of interviews are the

1. Phone interview

2. Face-to-face interview

3. Group interview

4. Meal interview

Phone Interview

The phone interview is the most common interview as it is usually the first step in the interview process. The objective of a phone interview is for the recruiter or hiring manager to learn a little more about your background in order to properly screen out the candidates who do not match the position specifications. Position specifications are generally internal documents that highlight what skills are needed for an open position. The interviewer will use these specifications to determine whether a candidate has the appropriate qualifications for a given position. Here are a few tips I recommend for phone interviews.

- When the phone interview is scheduled, ask the interviewer if you can be the one to initiate the call. For example, if the interviewer calls you and schedules the interview for 3 p.m. Tuesday, ask if you can call them. Doing so reduces your stress level prior to the interview. If you can call them, you are ready for the interview as soon as you begin dialing the phone. If you wait for them to call you, you will be stressed fifteen minutes prior to the call waiting for them to call you. However, if the interview is scheduled for 3 p.m., you need to call at 3 p.m. on the dot.

- Dress professionally for the phone interview. When you are dressed professionally, you feel and act much more professional.

- Prepare the house or apartment for the interview. Let everyone know that you will be on the phone for an interview.

- Sit at a table where you can utilize your notes or stand near your notes. Standing can help project your voice, which illustrates confidence. The phone interview is like an open book test. You can have everything in front of you. Just make sure you do not flip through your notes on every question. However, feel free to have a copy of your résumé in front of you to refer to your background and employment details. In addition, you can have a company's annual report and any marketing materials you may have gathered during the informational interview. Be familiar with this information already. Don't try to read the annual report while you are in the process of the interview.

- Never conduct a phone interview on a cell phone as you may lose the connection during the call.

- Disable call waiting. If you forget, never click over to answer a call on call waiting. It is perceived as rude.

- Make sure you ask at least three to five questions about the company at the end of the interview. If you did your research prior to the interview, you can ask questions about your findings—for example, "I noticed during my research that XYZ Company is planning to grow by 10 percent next year. Where do you feel that growth will come from?"

- At the end of the phone interview, make sure you close with a few questions about your interaction with the company. "Did I answer your questions to your satisfaction? Do my qualifications match your position criteria?" If they answer yes, ask about next steps and expectations of the face-to-face interview. If the interviewer answers no, meaning you did not match the position criteria, ask for constructive criticism and listen. Do not defend yourself. Use the information you gather for improving your next interview. I would just thank the interviewer for his or her time and wish them the best of luck.

A typical phone interview lasts approximately twenty to forty minutes. The topics most likely to be covered are your background and experience, your education, your job desires (what type of job you want), your salary expectations, your strengths as they apply to the job, and your perception of your weaknesses. A sample of an interviewer's phone interview script appears in Figure 16.

Figure 16

Telephone Interview Script

Candidate name_____ Date_____

Where did you hear about the position/company?

_____

Current company_____ Dates_____

Why are you looking for a new job? (Reasons for leaving previous positions/employment gaps)

Current Compensation:
    Base:
    Bonus:
    Benefits:
    Desired:

What type of position are you interested in?

Commuting/travel issues (if applicable):

Education:
    School:
    Degree:
    Certifications:
    Desire to continue:

What is your current availability?

Are you interviewing anywhere else?
    Status:
    Desire:

What are the most important factors in accepting a new job?

Work experience:
- Software languages, if applicable
- Lead role (leadership)
- Level of contacts (sales)
- Size of accounts (sales)
- Amount sold in revenue (sales)
- Quality testing methods (QA)
- Sales methods (sales)
- Work environment (team)

Face-to-Face Interview

The second most common interview is the face-to-face interview. This interview should be viewed as a formal interview. This interview takes place with either the hiring manager for the position (your future boss) or by a human resource person. Whoever it is, make sure you follow the interview guidelines to help you prepare. This section is designed to provide a basic overview of a face-to-face interview in the context of the types of interviews you may face. Later in the chapter, we explore the details of your formal interview.

Wear a formal suit for all interviews. While some companies dress in business casual for daily business, do not wear business casual during the interview process. Wear a professional suit to make a positive first impression. When arriving for the interview, be sure to show up fifteen minutes ahead of the scheduled time, which gives you time to mentally prepare and to have one last look at yourself in the restroom before the interview. Remember to be personable with the receptionist. In some companies, the receptionist is an important part of the interview process. The company may want to find out how you treat others in the company and how you make a first impression. I recommend introducing yourself and explaining that you were scheduled for an interview with Mr. or Ms. _____ at 3 p.m. The receptionist also knows a lot about the company.

You may want to ask him or her questions about the company if you have time and the receptionist appears receptive.

You need to prepare a few items ahead of time and bring them to the interview in a leather portfolio. You should have three printed copies of your résumé on professional résumé paper. Do not bring photocopied résumés. You also should have three reference letters. Make sure you have a recommendation letter from your previous boss, a professor from your school (if you are a recent graduate), and a professional peer. You should also consider an electronic copy of your résumé on disk. This way you can be certain that the interviewer or hiring manager has an electronic copy of your résumé to share with others.

You should also have any information required for a job application. When you arrive at the interview, you likely are going to be completing an application. You should have information about your previous employment, including the dates worked, address and phone number, previous manager's name, and salary information. Bring these documents with you so that the application details are not something you are struggling to remember. You have a lot of things on your mind to consider, and the last thing you should have to worry about is an application. Figure 17 shows a sample application.

Figure 17

APPLICATION FOR EMPLOYMENT

PLEASE PRINT

Equal access to programs, services, and employment is available to all persons. Those applicants requiring reasonable accommodation to the application and/or interview process should notify a representative of the Human Resources Department.

Position(s) applied for_____ Date of application _____

Name _____ Social Security # _____

(Last Name, First Name & Middle Name)

Address _____

(Street, City, State, Zip Code)

Telephone #_____ Mobile/Beeper/Other Phone #_____

E-mail Address _____

If you are under 18, and it is required, can you furnish a work permit? ❑ Yes ❑ No

If no, please explain_____

Have you ever been employed here before? ❑ Yes ❑ No

If yes, give dates and positions _____

Are you legally eligible for employment in this country? ❑ Yes ❑ No

Date available for work_____ What is your desired salary range?_____

Type of employment desired ❑ Full-Time ❑ Part-Time ❑ Temporary
                                              ❑ Seasonal ❑ Educational Co-Op

Are you able to meet the attendance requirements of the position? ❑ Yes ❑ No

Have you ever pled "guilty" or "no contest" to or been convicted of a crime?
❑ Yes ❑ No

If yes, please provide date(s) and details _____

ANSWERING "YES" TO THESE QUESTIONS DOES NOT CONSTITUTE AN AUTOMATIC BAR TO EMPLOYMENT. FACTORS SUCH AS DATE OF THE OFFENSE, SERIOUSNESS AND NATURE OF THE VIOLATION, REHABILI-TATION, AND POSITION APPLIED FOR WILL BE TAKEN INTO ACCOUNT.

Driver's license number if driving is an essential job function _____ State ____

Employment History _____

Provide the following information of your past three (3) employers, assignments, or volunteer activities, starting with the most recent.

From	To	Employer	Telephone #
Starting Job Title/ Final Job Title		Address	
Immediate Supervisor and Title		Summarize the Nature of Work Performed and Job Responsibilities	
May We Contact for Reference? ❑ Yes ❑ No ❑ Later			
Reason for Leaving		Hourly Rate/Salary Start $ Per Final $ Per	

From	To	Employer	Telephone #
Starting Job Title/ Final Job Title		Address	
Immediate Supervisor and Title		Summarize the Nature of Work Performed and Job Responsibilities	
May We Contact for Reference? ❑ Yes ❑ No ❑ Later			
Reason for Leaving		Hourly Rate/Salary Start $ Per Final $ Per	

From	To	Employer	Telephone #
Starting Job Title/ Final Job Title		Address	
Immediate Supervisor and Title		Summarize the Nature of Work Performed and Job Responsibilities	
May We Contact for Reference? ❑ Yes ❑ No ❑ Later			
Reason for Leaving		Hourly Rate/Salary Start $ Per Final $ Per	

AN EQUAL OPPORTUNITY EMPLOYER

Skills and Qualifications

Summarize any training, skills, licenses, and/or certificates that may qualify you as being able to perform job-related functions in the position for which you are applying.

_____

_____

_____

_____

Educational Background (if job related)

Name and Location	Number of Years Completed	Did You Graduate?	Course of Study
High School			
College		Major Degree	
Other			

References

Name	Telephone	Number of Years Known

Applicant Statement

I certify that all information I have provided in order to apply for and secure work with the employer is true, complete, and correct.

I understand that any information provided by me that is found to be false, incomplete, or misrepresented in any respect will be sufficient cause to (i) cancel further consideration of this application or (ii) immediately discharge me from the employer's service, whenever it is discovered.

I expressly authorize, without reservation, the employer, its representatives, employees, or agents to contact and obtain information from all references (personal and professional), employers, public agencies, licensing authorities and educational institutions and to otherwise verify the accuracy of all information provided by me in this application, résumé, or job interview. I hereby waive any and all rights and claims I may have regarding the employer, its agents, employees, or representatives, for seeking, gathering, and using such information in the employment process and all other persons, corporations, or organizations for furnishing such information about me.

I understand that the employer does not unlawfully discriminate in employment and no question on this application is used for the purpose of limiting or excusing any applicant from consideration for employment on a basis prohibited by applicable local, state, or federal law.

I understand that this application remains current for only 30 days. At the conclusion of that time, if I have not heard from the employer and still wish to be considered for employment, it will be necessary to reapply and fill out a new application.

If I am hired, I understand that I am free to resign at any time, with or without cause and without prior notice, and the employer reserves the same right to terminate my employment at any time, with or without cause and without prior notice, except as may be required by law. This application does not constitute an agreement or contract for employment for any specified period or definite duration. I understand that no supervisor or representative of the employer is authorized to make any assurances to the contrary and that no implied, oral, or written agreements contrary to the foregoing express language are valid unless they are in writing and signed by the employer's president.

I also understand that if I am hired, I will be required to provide proof of identity and legal authority to work in the United States and that federal immigration laws require me to complete an I-9 Form in this regard.

DO NOT SIGN UNTIL YOU HAVE READ THE ABOVE APPLICANT STATEMENT.

I certify that I have read, fully understand, and accept all terms of the foregoing Applicant Statement.

Signature of Applicant _____ Date _____/_____/_____

You should be prepared to complete this type of information when you arrive for the interview.

Once you arrive at your interview, remember to make a positive first impression. You should make sure you look and feel like you can take on the world. Make sure you follow the guidelines in the "Dressing the Part" chapter of this book. The face-to-face interview is an opportunity for you to sell yourself in person. Take your time and think about every answer. The time frame for a face-to-face interview is typically one hour. However, in some cases, they may ask that you interview with different people from the company. I recommend that you have at least five questions typed and prepared to ask during the interview. Make sure your questions show that you did your homework, such as: "I noticed in your annual report that you were planning to expand into Europe. What is driving that decision?" You may also take notes during the interview, but be sure to ask the interviewer for permission before you start taking notes. Finally, the interview is just a meeting between two people. They are evaluating you on your personality, cultural fit, experience, education, skills, and knowledge. Be yourself and best of luck.

Group Interview

The third type of interview is a group interview. Although group interviews are not all that common, you should know some details in case you encounter such an interview. The group interview is much like the face-to-face interview except that two to three people are in the room at the same time. This interview is common with very stressful jobs such as a social worker or police officer. The group interview evaluates how you deal with the stress of a group setting and how you deal with multiple questions. The best guideline is for you to stay calm and answer each question much like a face-to-face interview. Take your time and speak to each person in the room. Ask each interviewer a question at the end of the interview to show that you are engaged and interested. This time also presents an opportunity for you to evaluate the personality of the company by talking with each person and watching their interaction and nonverbal behavior.

The most important guideline is to take your time and think through each question, which will be a bit more stressful than a one-on-one interview. Your preparation is critical. In some cases, you can ask the recruiter who is scheduling your interview what type of interview you can expect. If you follow these guidelines, you will be very prepared for whatever type of interview you face.

Meal Interview

The final type of interview is the meal interview. The meal interview typically takes place during lunch hours and involves the hiring manager. Either the hiring manager is interviewing you during lunch because his/her schedule is too busy or the manager wants to see how you interact in public. Whatever the reason, these guidelines can help you do well.

The first guideline is to make sure you eat before the interview. That advice probably sounds silly considering the interview will be held during a meal, but because you will be doing most of the talking, the last thing you want to be doing is staring at the manager's sandwich with your mouth salivating because you are hungry.

The second rule is to bring money or a credit card with you just in case the manager does not pay. That typically won't happen, but it is always best to be prepared.

The third guideline is to order something that is easy to eat. One of the main concerns that stress out job candidates on meal interviews is what to order. You do not want to eat something that is sloppy when you are the candidate looking to impress. In addition, you also don't want to order something outrageously expensive. My recommendation is for you to ask the interviewer what meal(s) they recommend. This question eliminates your worry about cost because they are recommending the dish. A safe bet is to order some sort of salad or chicken entrée. Avoid ordering anything that needs to be eaten with your hands.

The fourth guideline is to never order alcohol. Even if the interviewer orders a double shot of whiskey with a martini chaser, never follow suit. The interviewer's action could be a test to see if you would drink on the job. In addition, drinking impairs your responses, no matter what your tolerance. Just kindly say, "No thanks, I will have the lemonade." Treat this meeting as formal as a face-to-face interview, but make sure you interact with the server as well as the host when you are being seated. Remember, the interviewer is also evaluating your behavior in public.

Most importantly, make sure you have good manners when you are having lunch. Do not eat with your mouth open, for example. Finally, take along your portfolio with your résumé and questions inside, just like for the face-to-face interview.

Interview Topics

Now that we have explored the types of interviews you could face, let's review the type of topics that the interviews cover. As you prepare for the interviews and do your research on your target companies, make sure you think about your answers to the following topics.

Experience

One obviously important topic is your experience as it applies to the position for which you are interviewing. Make sure you fully understand the position's qualifications as stated in the job posting, on the employer's Web site, or through a position description you gathered during your research. Be prepared for questions such as, "Why should I hire you for this position?" "What makes you more qualified than the other candidates that we are interviewing?" or " Relate your past experience to this position." Try to review your résumé as well as the accomplishments list that you developed earlier in the book. Apply your accomplishments to these types of questions.

Company knowledge

The second topic that might be covered is company knowledge. The interviewer's questions would probably include "Why do you want to work for XYZ Company?" or "Tell me about my company." Make sure you research the company thoroughly. Mention the Web site, the annual report, and information you gathered during your informational interview. Remember, many candidates are applying for this same job. You need to differentiate yourself by showing that you did your homework.

Communication skills

The third topic is your communication skills, which are evaluated during the interview. My research shows that the most important attribute a candidate can have is the ability to communicate. Interviewers might ask questions such as "Tell me about a time when you had to give bad news to a person" or "Tell me how you would sell my company to your friends." Remain confident. Confidence shows through and allows you to communicate in an effective manner. The interviewer is looking for confidence, knowledge, and proper grammar. Practice with family and friends.

Teamwork

The fourth topic is teamwork. The interviewer is evaluating your ability to function in a team environment. In today's business world, many companies are focusing on teams as part of their cultures. When you are preparing for the interview, think about when you were part of a team. What was the task? Who made up the team? How did the team interact? Who was the team leader? Most importantly, what was the outcome? If you are new to the workforce, these experiences can be related to high school sports, club activities, or group projects at school. The interviewer is looking for your attitude toward teamwork and your successes and failures in team settings. Think about your most memorable team experience and prepare your thoughts to respond to this topic during the interview.

Leadership experience

The fifth topic is your leadership experience. The interviewer is evaluating your potential as a leader and is using your past leadership examples as a gauge for the evaluation. This topic can also draw on your high school, club, or group activities. Try to remember when you were put in charge of a project, task, or team. How did you approach the task? Were you a motivational leader or a leader who earned the group's respect by doing? Did you delegate the activities and follow a project plan, or did you allow the team to choose the tasks to achieve the goal at hand? The interviewer looks for these types of things. When you think about your experiences, write them down on a piece of paper. Try to choose the one experience that could apply to the position you are interviewing for and expand your thoughts on that experience. This preparation, which your competition might not be considering, allows you to be a bit more prepared for the interview, thus reducing your stress and increasing your chances of success.

Educational experience

Another important interview topic is your educational experience. The interviewer is looking for information about your decision to attend your particular college or university, as well as why you chose your specific major and your knowledge within that major. Prepare for questions about your favorite and least favorite classes as well as your favorite professor and reasons for all your answers. The reason I ask these types of questions in my interviews is to evaluate what motivates you. If I know that you liked a class because it was always new and exciting, I can feel more comfortable placing you in a job that challenges you and subjects you to frequent change. If I know that you are motivated by a teacher who pushes you to do better, I would want to place you in a position that has that style of manager or leader. Finally, knowing why you chose your major helps me evaluate your motivation. If I know that you are motivated by money, for example, I may want to put you in a sales job.

Your college major is important as a backdrop of knowledge. However, you should know that only 30 percent of students actually end up working in their major after college. The major is important because it gives you a foundation of knowledge. As an employer, I am not hiring you to be an accountant because you majored in accounting and are a solid accountant. I am hiring you because you can scale up. You have a baseline of knowledge upon which I can build. Most college students do not have work experience, which is okay. However, if you have a solid foundation, you will most likely succeed.

Logic

A characteristic that interviewers are looking for is logical thinking. Take your time and think about each question. Do not try to answer with words you think the interviewer wants to hear. Think about the questions, and answer them to the best of your ability. Remember, you have done a significant amount of preparation for the interview. Take your time and show what you have done. Do not, however, just ramble on and on. Make sure you answer the questions they ask. Read their nonverbal signals and finish your answer. Remember, interviewers put their pants on one leg at a time just like the rest of us. They are people looking to hire a person who matches the requirements. If you prepare for the interview using these guidelines, you will excel and land the job you are looking for.

Sample interview questions

Now that you are aware of some typical interview topics, consider some examples of questions that an interviewer may ask you. Each set of questions is contained within a general area of knowledge that the interviewer is evaluating. Below the questions, I have included the evaluation criteria that each set of questions uncovers about the candidate. (Note that while these questions apply to past jobs, they can also be answered relative to time in school or college.)

Collaboration and Teamwork

- How have you gone about developing a cohesive, high-functioning team atmosphere in the past? How would you do it at my company?

- In your last position, how would your previous coworkers describe you? What was it like to work with you? What would they say about your collaboration and teamwork style?

- Give examples of how you've brought out the best in others in a team environment.

- Tell me about a time when you had to deal with a difficult coworker. What made him/her difficult? What did you do? What was the outcome?

Evaluation Criteria:

Articulates a history of succeeding in a team environment.

Demonstrates a history of success working in teams.

Makes other team members better.

Handles conflict among team members well.

Communication

- What are your strengths with respect to communication skills? What aspects of communication would you like to further develop?

- If we ask your last boss, how will he or she describe your writing skills? What are your strengths and developmental needs in this regard?

- In what ways was written communication required in your previous jobs? What materials or samples of your writing best demonstrate your writing skills? Describe the technical documents you've written in your past two jobs.

- How would your colleagues and/or boss describe your communication skills?

Evaluation Criteria:

Articulates an ability to write effectively.

Demonstrates a history of strong communication skills.

Speaks clearly and intelligently.

Presents self well in terms of conveying important concepts and ideas.

Influencing

- In your current job, describe a situation where you were required to persuade or influence someone to your point of view. What was your approach? How did the other person respond? What happened?

- How would you describe your style of persuasion? What are your strengths? In what ways do you need to become more effective? How do people typically respond to your style of persuasion?

- Think of someone who comes to mind as being especially persuasive. Who? Why is this person persuasive? What have you learned from him or her? How has this person influenced your style?

- Give an example of where you had to bring the best of your persuasion skills into play. What did you do? What skills did you use?

Evaluation Criteria:

Emphasizes importance of selling ideas and gaining other people's buy-in.

Establishes rapport during interview.

Comes across as persuasive and able to sell ideas.

Utilizes appropriate styles of persuasion.

Achievement Focus

- What would people who know you well say about your ability to overcome setbacks, adversity, or failure? Be specific and give some examples.

- What has been your greatest personal success regarding your academic or professional career? Why do you consider this to be your greatest success?

- Discuss your key accomplishments in your last two positions (professional or academic). How have you added value in key roles you've held?

- In your last two jobs or internships, discuss your performance expectations and goals.

- Describe your performance in relation to these expectations and goals.

- Describe some important setbacks or failures that you've experienced. What did you do in response to these situations?

- If you were to create a list of career highlights, what would be on it? Why?

Evaluation Criteria

Paints a clear picture of achievement and personal successes.

Is clearly driven to succeed.

Demonstrates more achievement focus than most.

Demonstrates the ability to overcome adversity.

Bias of Action

- What would people who know you well say about your level of initiative and the extent to which you know when action is a priority? Be specific and provide some examples.

- Give me an indication of the extent to which you are comfortable making decisions on your own without input from your boss. Convince me you are able to make decisions and take action on your own.

- Do you react better to a lot of direction or minimal direction from others?

- What would your previous employer say about your ability to meet demands in a timely manner? Tell me about steps you've taken to ensure that required work is completed.

- How would you rate your ability to remain persistent and follow through on work commitments? Give me some examples that support your assessment.

- What would your previous boss say about your willingness to take responsibility for your work, and to what extent would he or she say you took ownership of your projects or commitments?

- In your current or previous jobs, on what occasions did you feel you should consult with your boss before proceeding with some action? When did you feel it was proper to act on your own?

- Describe a time during your past two positions or internships in which you went above and beyond what it took to get the job done. Describe the situation and what you did.

Evaluation Criteria:

Goes above and beyond the call of duty.

The candidate is comfortable with making decisions.

Knows when to make decisions and when to solicit input from others.

Takes ownership for his or her work.

Customer Focus

- In your view, what are the ways in which you directly impact the satisfaction of customers (internal or external)? Tell me about how you did this in your last two jobs.

- What do you think are the key needs and expectations of our customers?

- In your most recent position, whom did you consider your primary customers? In your view, what were their needs or expectations?

- Describe a time when you provided an exceptional level of customer service. What specifically did you do? What were the outcomes? Why was it exceptional?

- What would your previous boss say about your commitment to satisfying the customer? In what ways did you fall short of providing excellent customer service?

- In your view, how can the level of customer service provide a competitive advantage over my company's competitors (or, how did customer service provide a competitive advantage in your last two roles)?

- Describe the benefits of good customer service. What are the advantages and what are the drawbacks to poor customer service?

Evaluation Criteria:

Understands the importance of customer service.

Articulates a history of satisfying the customer.

Practices good customer service.

Understands customer service as a competitive advantage.

Flexibility and Versatility

- Talk about an experience you had where you needed to change your plan or approach to work on a project. What led to the change, and how did you react?

- What would previous supervisors say about your capability to handle work requirements that are not routine or which change from day to day?

- In your previous work, did you encounter multiple demands that needed to be met simultaneously? Talk about how you approached this work to meet these demands.

- Describe a job or work situation that caused you to feel a lot of stress. Were you able to resolve the situation, and how did you do so?

Evaluation Criteria:
Conveys experience with changing work demands.

Describes experience, indicating ability to multitask.

Indicates ability to shift focus/effort as needed.

Suggests ability to react positively to change or stressful situations.

Integrity

- Define what integrity means to you. How do you demonstrate integrity, both professionally and personally?

- Give me some examples of how you have built trust or earned the respect of others. What kind of reputation do you have with your peers? What would they say if I asked them?

- What will your previous one or two bosses say about your integrity? Further, what will they say about the extent to which you met commitments that you made to others and did what you said you would do?

- Describe a time when you lost the trust of coworkers. What happened? What did you do? Why? What did you learn from that?

Evaluation Criteria:

Articulates a history of professional integrity.

Understands the importance of trust in an organization.

Demonstrates a history of personal integrity.

Follows through on all commitments to others.

Business Focus

- In your current or previous position, describe to me how the company operated. How did it make money? What service did it provide to its customer base? How did your company's products or services provide business solutions for customers?

- Describe your understanding of my company from a business perspective.

- When evaluating proposed projects or products, what criteria do you use to determine if they are worthwhile or if they will generate a good return on investment?

- In your past role, describe some of the key functions,

divisions, or departments and what division you worked in. How did the various divisions affect each other?

- In your previous one or two positions, how did you (or your position in general) specifically impact either the organization or department's bottom line? What actions had an impact on the organization's performance?

Evaluation Criteria:

Demonstrates functional excellence.

Identifies drivers of business growth and profitability.

Demonstrates knowledge of my company's business and various business functions.

Creative and Innovative

- On a scale from 1 to 10, rate your level of creativity and innovative thinking. Why did you rate yourself there? Give specifics and justify your rating.

- When was the last time you had a creative or innovative idea. What was it?

- How would your past one or two bosses evaluate your creativity or ability to think outside the box when solving challenging problems?

- Tell me about a time where you developed a new procedure or method that improved productivity. Provide specifics. What did you do? What was the outcome?

- Talk about the importance of creativity and innovation in a company like my company.

- If I were to observe you on the job for a couple of weeks and saw you at your creative best, what would I see you do?

Evaluation Criteria:

Demonstrates the ability to think outside the box.

Appreciates the importance of creativity and innovation at my company.

Articulates a history of creative and innovative thinking in past roles.

Adds value through creative and innovative thinking.

Aptitude

- What would your previous boss say about your ability to pick up things quickly and to learn new technologies, products, or services? Why would he or she say this? Give some examples from your past two positions.

- What do you do to ensure continuous learning and to stay abreast of key developments in your field?

- If someone were to ask you why you are an expert about your job, what would you tell them?

- What do you do to stay informed about new products and services relevant to your job/career?

Evaluation Criteria:

Demonstrates technical expertise.

Articulates an ability to learn quickly.

Understands the key products and services relevant to my company.

Stays current on developments in the field.

Multitasking and Prioritizing

- Describe a time when you were working on two or more projects simultaneously. What did you do to ensure that you would accomplish both tasks accurately and on time? Give some specific examples.

- What would your previous boss say about your ability to handle many responsibilities at one time and to prioritize effectively among them?

- When you have many things going on at one time, how do you prioritize, and where do you focus your attention?

Evaluation Criteria:

Demonstrates the ability to balance multiple priorities at one time without compromising quality.

Articulates a history of meeting multiple commitments simultaneously.

Appropriately prioritizes tasks to best maximize productivity.

Can handle multiple tasks concurrently.

Strategic Thinking

- Have you ever participated in a strategic planning process? What did you learn from that experience?

- What was the business strategy of your former employer; in your opinion, was it an effective one? Why or why not?

- What are some key strategic issues that my company needs to consider as it moves forward? What about the particular group you are moving into: what are its strategic issues?

- Have you ever been involved in a disciplined approach to strategic planning? Please describe. What was the situation? What was your involvement? What was the outcome?

Evaluation Criteria:

Aligns goals with corporate strategy and vision.

Anticipates business challenges and opportunities.

Sees the big picture.

Understands my company's basic corporate strategy.

Preparation/Practice for the Interview

Now that we have discussed the types of interviews, interview topics, and potential interview questions you might face, it is time for practice and final preparation for your formal interview.

The spotlight is focused on you as the star during the interview. The interview is also a time for the company to be in the spotlight. The interview is a chance to learn about them as much as it is for them to learn about you. This time is for you to shine and show your stuff and to give it your best.

Three basic stages are associated with the interview: preparation, the actual interview, and follow-up.

How to prepare for the interview

The first step of preparing for an interview is to review your internal and external assessment as discussed earlier in the book. Consider your personal and professional goals. Ask yourself some basic questions regarding your personal and professional life.

1) What are your goals in three years?

2) What are your goals in five to ten years?

3) What are your strengths/weaknesses?

4) What is your greatest accomplishment? What did you learn from this?

5) What was your biggest defeat? What did you learn?

6) What did you like/dislike about your major?

7) What are your thoughts about relocation?

8) What is your desired salary?

9) What are your five greatest attributes?

10) What do you value in life?

Even if these questions are not asked in the interview, they help you further analyze your goals and therefore allow you to answer the interviewer's questions more easily and thoroughly.

Another action that might help your interview go smoothly is to practice. Talk in the mirror, to a friend, or in the shower. You need to prepare for interview questions such as, "What are your greatest strengths? Weaknesses? Greatest accomplishment? Why do you want to work here? Why should we hire you?"

The next step is researching the company. Make sure you research the company thoroughly before you walk through its door. Know how long the company has been in existence, its growth in the past five years, how many people it employs, what it actually does, and most importantly, what you will do for the company. Two of the biggest complaints that interviewers have are that candidates are unprepared or know little about the company.

Ask yourself how well you fit the company's culture and what your impact on this company would be. Why should they hire you? What can you bring to this company? Look at its strengths and match them to yours. Everything you know about the company prior to interviewing contributes to your competitive edge. Do you think the other applicants for this position are doing extensive research on their potential employers? You need to make yourself stand out. If the interviewer asks, "Have you ever worked in small teams?" and you know that the company prides itself in small-team orientation projects, you can relate your experiences directly to the small-group behavior.

Remember, interviewers are looking for someone they like and who fits in well with the ideals and goals of the firm. Do not make things up or exaggerate. People know when you're lying, and you will lose not only your credibility with that interviewer, but more likely the job offer. These interviewers talk. They are all part of the interview team. Don't burn your bridges. Always be honest, and that integrity will remain with you.

Give yourself the competitive advantage and learn as much about a company as you can. Everything you learn about a company can be used. Even if you don't get the job with firm A, you may find that you have an interview with or even become employed by that firm's competitor at company B. You already know the weaknesses, strengths, and products of company A from your research. You are now in a position to intelligently discuss the industry and the two particular competitors.

Once the research is complete and you feel confident, the next step is the interview itself.

The First Formal Interview

The most important thing to remember about an interview is that you need to be confident and view this meeting as networking. In addition, you are the subject matter expert about yourself. Use this to your advantage and remain confident.

Interviewers are looking for the perfect people for their firms; you are looking for a job. They have pressure on them to perform for their firms, just as you are under pressure to perform for yourself. You have a lot in common with this new contact. This person is in a field that you enjoy. This person was in the same shoes as you at one time. They researched, interviewed, and were nervous. Go into the interview with the idea that no matter what happens, at least you will emerge knowing a little more about interviewing and with one more professional contact. The interviewer can be part of your network at a later date.

Remember that interviewing is a two-way street. The interviewer is trying to find out what they are getting. Who is this person? Why is this person here? Can this person do the job? Will this person stay with the firm? Will this person fit in with the corporate culture already in place? In addition, you are testing yourself and learning if this job is what you are looking for. Will I be challenged? Will I learn? Do I fit into the company? Does the company fit me? These types of questions are the basic reasons you are interviewing. This time is yours to show your stuff, to shine in the spotlight, and to possibly gain a new friend. You may even find that you do not want to work for this company. Either way, you will walk away a better, more knowledgeable person, no matter what the outcome.

An interview is just two people talking to and about each other. We all like to talk about ourselves. You have earned the right to shine and to show what you are made of. Welcome the opportunity to challenge yourself and to stand above your competition to get the job.

Be sure to arrive on time for your interview. Try to arrive about ten to fifteen minutes early if you can, because punctuality shows that you are responsible and dependable. Catch up on the latest news if you have not done so already. Pick up the morning paper or watch the evening news the night before. This topic may break the ice in the interview and illustrate that you are knowledgeable about current events. In addition, you may want to think of some items of discussion to break the ice yourself. For instance, you may notice the firm's new advertising campaign on television and comment on it. Try to stay away from political or emotionally charged issues.

You should also prepare about five questions to ask the interviewer. These questions could be about his or her position, the company's growth potential, or how the open position affects the long-term strategy of the company. Have these questions typed. You may want to ask the interviewer if he or she would mind if you took notes during the interview. Sometimes you may want to write a few ideas, questions, or answers down during the interview to ask later.

Greet the interviewer with a firm handshake (men and women), which gives a strong, confident first impression to the interviewer. During the interview, use good posture and sit up straight, which demonstrates confidence and pride. Also, be sure to always look the interviewer in the eye. This shows your eagerness to learn and your ability to listen.

You are most likely going to be asked questions about yourself. However, they will often be in-depth questions to illustrate how you handle various types of situations. In fact, you are likely to be asked when you have demonstrated some specific ability. At this point, your experiences in organizations or internships can help you the most. Use what you have learned from your past experiences to sell yourself. Make sure you think about each question before you answer it. You do not want to be too aggressive and seem overbearing. There is no time limit, so take your time, listen, and answer the questions thoroughly.

You are likely to get some tough questions during the interview. Commonly, interviewees are asked to give their greatest strengths and weaknesses. Employers may look for all different answers here, but they are often curious as to how you view yourself and what you are doing to work on problems. Focus on the strengths that are useful in the workplace, such as being a team player, goal-oriented, or a problem-solver. Be ready to defend these strengths with examples of situations when you demonstrated these abilities. The weaknesses are a bit more difficult. You must stay away from weaknesses that will have anything to do with the prospective job, such as being stubborn, or fear of speaking or communicating your feelings. Focus on correctable weaknesses such as saying, "I'm not as organized as I would like to be, so I have recently purchased a daily planner." That type of answer shows that you know your weakness, that it is fixable, and that you are working to correct it. Another such weakness might be your lack of delegation abilities. You can correct this by prioritizing and delegating tasks to others. Whatever your weakness, be sure to have some way of correcting it, and inform the interviewer that you are doing just that.

Be prepared for a question about specific examples of how you have handled various situations. To prepare for this, you may want to sit down a week before the interview and think about some situations in which you accomplished a goal or faced a conflict, failed and learned from it, and made a tough choice. Be ready to share a leadership role you have had.

Under no circumstances should you discuss possible salary figures in your first interview. An interviewer may ask what type of salary you are looking for. A good response is a brief statement such as, "I am considering many opportunities with many firms. What is the salary range that accompanies this position?" Salary negotiations are not dealt with until you have an actual job offer, which usually does not come until after several interviews. Once the job has been offered, try to ask for a few days to decide. Do not jump at it. In those few days, you can evaluate the job offer, responsibilities, corporate culture, and opportunities for growth.

After you have answered the interviewer's questions, you then have the opportunity to ask some of your own. Try to use questions that relate to the research you uncovered. Use the questions you wrote prior to the interview or ask questions that you have thought of since the interview started. Although you have written your questions on paper, you should still have them committed to memory. Here are some examples of good interview questions:

1) Through my research, I have found that XYZ Corporation has grown 23 percent in the last year. What steps is the firm taking to ensure this continued growth (new products, mergers, strategic alliances)?

2) What type of training programs do you offer to new employees?

3) What is the evaluation/measurement process for this position?

4) What type of person are you looking for?

5) What are some of the goals of the firm for the next five years?

Apply the answers to these questions to your employment decisions. Remember, you are interviewing the company as much as they are interviewing you. Later, you can list all the pros and cons that were revealed during your interviews and evaluate the material to make a fully educated decision about the company where you would like to work.

The second interview

Once the first interview is complete, the interviewer will probably want you to return for a second interview, which is very common. During the second interview, you might meet with a new set of people, including the team with which you would be working. You may also meet with the individuals who interact with this position. Focus on the same guidelines as the first interview. Take your time and use your research as strength. The second interview is also the time to discuss position and company specifics with the interviewer. I recommend asking detailed questions about the position as well as the company benefits.

Questions to help you better understand the job position:

Do you have a position description that I could review?

What are the roles and responsibilities of this position?

Can you explain the reporting structure and leadership structure for this position?

What are your expectations for the position?

What are the critical success factors for this position, and what would I need to accomplish to be successful?

Questions to ask in order to get a better understanding of the company's benefits:

What type of health care benefits does the firm offer?

What is the monthly insurance premium for single and/or married employees?

What type of life insurance does your firm offer?

Does the firm offer tuition reimbursement?

Does your firm offer a 401(k) retirement plan? If so, with what company?

Does your firm match my 401(k) contribution?

Does your company offer stock options?

What is the vacation policy?

Does this position have a bonus opportunity?

Does your firm have an orientation program?

Does your firm have a career development process?

Follow-Up After the Interviews

After you have completed the interviews, follow-up with a thank-you note. I recommend sending a thank-you note to everyone who interviewed you. I prefer a handwritten thank-you note because it differentiates you and is more thoughtful than a formal letter or an email. However, if you do not feel comfortable with a handwritten letter, send a well-written letter that references a few topics discussed during the interview as well as your interest in the position.

Next steps and expectations

You've had your interviews and followed up with a thank-you note. Your next step may be to wait. During this stage of the game, the key word is patience. Don't rush into anything and lose your chances or present yourself as being desperate. Often, the interviewer tells you during the interview the time frame for making a decision or what the hiring process entails. You may receive a call in a week or have literature sent

to you in the mail. The interviewer may set up the next interview right then (if applicable). Your job is to find out as many
details as you can about the process. If interviewers tell you
that they will call you in a week or so, try to ask them to spec-
ify a certain day. Also, ask if you could contact them if they
have not called you.

If you do not have any response in the amount of time
specified (or about two weeks if no time is specified), contact
them. At that point, ask the interviewer about the status of
the position and say that you want to confirm your interest
and your fit for the job. In addition ask them about their expectations regarding the decision, because you are interviewing with other organizations, which seem to be moving faster
than expected. This moment is a tricky one. You do not want
to push the hiring manager. However, at the same time you
want to show that you are in demand.

Rejection

Rejection is a part of life and something we all face at one
time or another. If you are not selected for a position, you will
most likely receive a letter to this effect. Such letters often say
that the company hired a "more qualified" candidate. However, the most qualified person is not necessarily who gets the
job; it is the person who knows how to market himself or her-
self, the person who knows what needs to be done to be successful during the interview. Make sure this person is you!
Learn from your mistakes and use this experience to gain this
knowledge. Henry Ford once said, "Failure is the opportunity
to begin again more intelligently." Do not let rejection dis-
courage you. Walt Disney was fired from a newspaper because
he lacked ideas. You need to continue to drive forward.

What should you do if you are turned down? First, don't
be discouraged. You may not have enjoyed working for that
company anyway. Perhaps the company saw that your personality did not fit its culture and that you would have ended

up leaving. Second, send a follow-up letter thanking the interviewer and the company for the opportunity to meet and interview with them. This step keeps your name on their minds. Third, be sure to continue to follow up with other companies to whom you have sent your résumé or have pending interviews. Keep your opportunities open. Finally, do not be afraid to interview with this company later. Often, you may not have met some qualifications such as practical experience. The next time you interview with this company, your competition for the position may be different, and the people making the decision to hire may be different as well.

Although this might be difficult, try to contact the interviewer who interviewed you and ask for advice on what you could do to improve. Remember, take constructive criticism and use it to your benefit. The interviewer may give you some beneficial points before you interview again. You can contact the person by phone or by sending them a letter. Either way, follow up with some of the interviewers whom you think may give you constructive feedback. Do not do this for every interview because you may get overwhelmed, which could lead to frustration and cause you to end the search process.

Sample questions for your follow-up letter after a rejection might be:

- "Could you please provide me with some areas in which you think I need improvement?"

- "Could you please provide me with constructive criticism to help me with the interview process?"

- "Could you give some pointers on interviewing and on things on which I could improve?"

We all need to learn from our mistakes, and the interviewing arena is perfect for learning about the business world from the ground floor.

Acceptance

The acceptance stage of the interviewing process is a process in itself. After all of the interviews are completed and they have chosen you, you receive an offer. This offer includes salary, benefits, vacation time, and so on. Discuss salary at this time. You should never discuss the subject of salary until they have placed an offer on the table. If the interviewer brings up the subject of salary at any time during the interview process, explain that you are researching many companies and at this point it is too soon to discuss any salary issues. However, if the recruiter pushes the issue about salary, make sure you have done your compensation research and provide a salary range. For example, "Based on my research, I have found that the base salary for a software developer with my skills is between $45,000 and $55,000 per year. What is the salary range for this position?"

You should consider two key salary issues once an offer is made. The first issue is based on the job you are considering. What is the average salary of that type of position? You can find this information on the Web or through the library or career center. However, you need to use your best judgment when reviewing salary figures on the Web. Make sure the figures are from a credible source. Far too often, salary figures are misrepresented on the Web to draw attention to an open position. In addition, you should find one of the many surveys conducted relating to this subject, which are categorized by industry and job title.

The second issue is negotiation. You should consider negotiation when applicable. If you are interviewing for an entry-level position, negotiating a salary may be very difficult or impossible. But if you feel that the salary is negotiable, go for it. Recognize that the employer will probably try to offer you as little money as possible. However, the employer may also have a set salary for an entry-level position. You probably need to make a judgment call. In most cases, the employer has a starting point and a maximum offer. This range fluctuates with position but can be negotiated. Do your homework and see what the average salary is for that position and even convey to the employer if the offer is below the average salary for that position. Be careful, though. If you are going for an entry-level position, negotiating room may be minimal.

Once the recruiter offers you the position, start the negotiation process. Consider the following negotiating tips.

- Never accept on the spot. When the interviewer offers you the job, tell the interviewer that you are very interested and you need to discuss it with your family. Even if you do not discuss it with your family, take time to think about the offer.

- Tell the interviewer that you will call him or her in a few days to provide an answer. This time is the best for negotiating. They are eager for you to accept. Negotiating over the phone can sometimes be your best strategy. Start with at least 10 percent above the offer. Typically, most interviewers have the authority to negotiate. When you call, explain to the interviewer that you are interested in the position, but you were expecting $x (10 percent above the offer). In some cases, the offer might be solid with no room to move. In that case, accept the position if it matches that company criteria you established at the front of this book.

- Keep in mind that you are negotiating the entire compensation package, not just base salary. Total compensation involves base salary, bonuses, and benefits. Keep this in perspective as you evaluate the offer.

Once you decide on the offer and want to accept, verbally accept and write an acceptance letter to the individual offering you the position. In addition, send a letter to all of the interviewers that you met with during the interview process, stating that you have accepted and are excited about working with the organization. This step is what the job search is all about: accepting a job offer. Remember that your reputation follows you everywhere you go, so you should never burn your bridges. Pay close attention to detail and follow up with diligence. Always give 100 percent, and ultimately you will succeed. An example of an acceptance letter is in Figure 18.

Figure 18

Acceptance Letter Example

January 3, 2003
John Doe
1011 North Norman St.
Cleveland, Ohio 99999

Greg Jones
Business Manager
XYZ Company
1111 White Road
Cleveland, Ohio 99998

Dear Greg:

This letter is to accept the position of sales associate with XYZ Company.

I am most excited about this opportunity. The position will be challenging and rewarding. I believe strongly in the corporate philosophy of XYZ Company and find the corporate culture most compatible.

Thank you for giving me this opportunity. I am confident that I can contribute significantly to the growth and success of XYZ Company.

Sincerely,

John Doe

Chapter 6

How to Succeed
in Your New Job

*"Success in business requires training and discipline and hard work.
But if you're not frightened by these things,
the opportunities are just as great today as they ever were."*

David Rockefeller

Congratulations! You have successfully completed your job search and found a great job. This chapter is designed to help you transition into your new job.

The first day is always the most exciting. As you settle into your new office, cube, or desk and receive your office supplies, use this book for one last piece of advice. Based on my experience and through my research, I have found the assimilation or orientation period for any new employee is the most critical time to make a positive first impression. The following detailed outline should assist you in making the transition as smooth as possible. This outline focuses on five parts of the organization you need to understand within your first ninety days of employment: company knowledge, position knowledge, product/service knowledge, process/political knowledge, and personal growth and effectiveness. Use this outline as a frame of reference when planning your days and scheduling time with your supporting leader or peers.

Company Knowledge

The first area of the business that you need to understand is the company itself. Do your best to fully understand the organization's history. How did the firm get started and who were its first customers? Try to learn the organization's mission statement and understand how it applies to the company, your team, and your specific position. Company values are also very important to understand. These guiding principles help illustrate how the culture is managed, decisions are made, and customers are serviced, and how the leadership group should perform. In addition, as part of any orientation program, understand how the organization is structured, which tells you who reports to whom and how groups within the company work together. An organizational structure is also a good starting point for you to develop your career development plan by identifying possible positions that interest you. Within the organizational structure, you need to understand the roles and responsibilities of your peers, managers, internal customers, and suppliers. Finally, you need to understand office infrastructure and logistics. If you need a new stapler, where do you go, and how do you order it? What are the software programs that you need to understand and use on a daily basis? These tools can include a scheduling and e-mail system, desktop publishing programs, and/or an internal customer relationship management system.

Use this list to help organize your learning and orientation of company knowledge.

Company or organizational history

Mission, values, and vision

Company culture

Organizational structure

People—roles and responsibilities

Office logistics/technology

Position Knowledge

The next phase of your orientation program is position knowledge. You need to understand and confirm the role and responsibilities of your position and understand the types of tasks for which you will be responsible. In addition, you should ask the human resources department for a copy of a position description. This document outlines your role and responsibilities and provides a framework of overall accountability.

Find out what current projects you are responsible for and the timing and expectations of these projects. I also recommend contacting a peer within the company for a position meeting. During this meeting, try to understand his or her role and responsibilities and position expectations. In some cases, I recommend conducting meetings with everyone with whom you would interact, including your internal suppliers or employees who supply you with information, content, and/or materials. You should also try to meet your internal customers. Who are your customers? What are their expectations of you and your role?

Finally you need to fully understand the critical success factors of your position. What will you be measured against to ensure your success? You should work with your managers to understand their expectations as well as the performance review process of your firm. To be successful, you need to understand how you are evaluated and reviewed for future promotions, salary raises, and so on.

Here is the list of topics for your position orientation.

Confirm role and responsibilities

Projects and tasks

Position expectations

Success measurements

Performance review process

Product/Service Knowledge

Once you feel that you have a solid understanding of the company knowledge and a full understanding of your position and organization's expectation, you need to develop a plan to learn about the products and services your company produces and sells. Do your best to fully understand all of the products and services within your firm and the history behind the products. In some cases, a cursory review of the products and services is sufficient. However, if you are dealing with these products on a daily basis, you need to fully understand the product specifications. The quicker you are up to speed, the more successful you will be. Make sure you document your learning through this phase. You will need to reference the information multiple times. If this learning takes place through a formal class or you have to schedule one-on-one time with a product expert, view this knowledge as an invaluable asset to your career growth within the firm. Read as much information within the internal and external Web sites as well as any marketing material you can gather. By understanding product features and attributes, you will be a more successful team player and well positioned within the firm for programs such as a fast-track program.

As part of this phase, you should also gain a better understanding of your market segments and the industries your firm targets. You also need to understand the firm's current customers as well as prospects. Develop a customer list and/or customer profile as you learn more. As you read about customers through case studies or press releases, save the information into a profile to reference later. Again, this information is an important asset to career growth.

Here is the list for your product/services orientation:

Product/service history

Products, features, and attributes

Product training program

Industries, customers, and prospects

Political/Process Knowledge

In preparing for a new career and settling into the firm, new employees often overlook one area: political/process knowledge. Any new employee experiences a period of initiation. In order to make a positive first impression, however, you need to understand the lay of the land so that you do not step into any land mines or on anyone's toes. The best way to approach this phase is to identify possible allies. This person can be the boss who hired you (although that does not tend to sit well with existing employees). Alternatively, this person could be a peer within your department or even outside the group.

The criteria you should use to identify potential allies are based on tenure, reputation, and influence. Often times, the person who has been there a long time and is well liked by many is the best person to partner with. Through my experiences, I have found that this step is often the most important. For example, I hired a senior executive in my firm who started his first day by challenging a peer in public. As with any organization, the news quickly spread, and this person's reputation was tarnished from day one. He was probably very good at his job, but no one gave him a chance in fear that he would turn on them as well. He lasted six months.

However, there is some good news. All new employees usually have a honeymoon period during which the company typically overlooks missteps or political mistakes. New employees are simply corrected or given advice to help them navigate through the political arena. Just think about when you started at a new school. The school had groups or cliques that spent their time building relationships as well as their reputation. Work is no different. Every company has processes, procedures, and norms. Some of these processes are well documented while others are silent norms and cultures. Do your best to understand your boundaries and the boundaries of your position and team. Spend your first ninety days learning, listening, and building relationships. This time and activity will serve you well in establishing a successful work environment.

Personal Effectiveness Knowledge

The final area where you need to focus your energies is on your own personal effectiveness. Use your performance review results to help improve your personal and professional performance. Perhaps target educational opportunities such as formal education, training, seminars, or certifications. As you grow within your position and firm, continually improve your personal effectiveness skills. Use the orientation process to help you formulate your strategy and specific steps that need to be done to build an individual career development plan.

A section earlier in this book outlined specific criteria you should consider when identifying your target companies. A formal career development program should be high on your list of desired factors for potential employers. In order for you to continually grow within your firm, you need to have a plan of action that should include expanding the breadth of your current role and identifying other potential positions within the firm you should target. Your career is your responsibility. Make sure you are continually improving your personal effectiveness skills. In some companies, you need to work with human resources, while in others the management team is well trained and expected to coach their employees. The following list of potential topics should help you get started in considering personal development.

Personal Effectiveness Skills

Business writing	Presentation skills
Listening skills	Project management
Interpersonal communication	Problem-solving skills
Time management	Creativity
Integrity and ethics	Flexibility/adaptability
Achievement orientation	Business acumen

Facilitation skills	Interviewing skills
Labor law	Conflict resolution
Building a high-performance team	Supervisory skills
Planning	Decision making
Project management	Process development
Coaching and mentoring	Financial management
Delegation and empowerment	Doing vs. leading
Industry knowledge	Organization skills
Technical knowledge	Position knowledge

As your progress in your career endeavors, make sure you continually improve your personal effectiveness. In my time as a professional career coach, I am often asked the question, "When will I know that it is time to move to another job, position, or company?" The advice I give to all of my clients is to focus on three aspects of your development: professional development, personal development, and financial development—in that order. I understand that the grass sometimes seems greener in other companies or in other positions. However, if you are focusing on these three developmental needs, you are managing your career effectively.

Professional Development

The first developmental area is your professional development. You should always be professionally challenged in your job. These challenges can come in many forms, such as a high quota, difficult learning curve, or the task of managing multiple people. Are you receiving opportunities to learn and grow within your position or role within the firm? Do you feel professionally stimulated with your projects, tasks, or contributions to the firm? Have you developed and communicated to your supporting leader a professional career development plan? I often ask these types of questions to professionals who consider leaving a position because they do not feel professionally challenged.

Personal Development

The second developmental area is your personal development. Do you enjoy your work? Do you like the people you work with? Does the company culture, team, or peer group that you work with personally stimulate you? Are your personal educational goals being met at your current company? You need to consider these types of questions when evaluating your personal developmental needs. You spend the majority of your life at work. Therefore, you need to personally enjoy the environment and be continually motivated to strive for excellence.

Financial Development

The final developmental area you need to evaluate is your financial development. Financial needs include base salary, bonus opportunities, and benefits provided by a firm. Through my experience, I realize that most people do not feel they are ever paid enough for the value they bring to a firm. However, do you feel you are paid a market-based salary for your position, education, experience level, and responsibility? Do you feel your bonus opportunity is realistic at your firm? Do you feel that the benefits offered at your firm match the market standards? Do you feel that your vacation time is adequate compared to the market? You need to evaluate these types of questions to review your financial developmental needs.

Often times, people change jobs or accept jobs strictly for financial reasons. Research conducted through organizational surveys, focus groups, and interviews shows that, for employees overall, financial rewards appear seventh among valued attributes of an organization. Based on my findings, the top-ten most valued attributes of an organization include:

1. Company stability

2. Organizational culture and environment

3. Employee morale

4. Leadership practices

5. Leader/employee relations

6. Performance feedback

7. Compensation and benefits

8. Growth and opportunity

9. Company innovation

10. Product quality

While an important aspect of a job, compensation is not considered the primary motivator for people who leave or accept new employment. As you are researching organizations, evaluating companies, or entertaining a job offer, make sure you are considering all aspects of the position and company. This holistic approach benefits you in the long run. If you are professionally challenged and personally motivated, the financial rewards will follow.

Afterword

Continue Knocking throughout Your Career!

"My interest is in the future because I am going to spend the rest of my life there."

Charles F. Kettering

As you continue to grow and prosper in your new job, maintain your focus on your career growth. The days of being employed by one company for your entire career are over. In today's fast-moving economy, the average job tenure is between three to five years; in other words, in three to five years, you will likely be looking for another opportunity. Therefore, you need to continue to build your network and sharpen your skills for your next career move. Keep this book as a resource for your next search, and implement the following guidelines as you manage your career.

Stay connected with your network.

As mentioned in the networking section in the "Resources to Utilize" chapter, you need to continually stay in contact with your network. Schedule time to make phone calls just to keep in touch. Schedule lunches with those key contacts to stay abreast of their career activities as well. As with any new job, you want to focus your energies on your tasks at hand, but do not forget to stay involved in your networking roundtables, industry associations, or social groups. Your network of family, friends, and business associates should continue to grow as you expand your career.

Remember, networking refers to a social activity typically utilizing reciprocal relationships to facilitate communication between people. Networking can be a very powerful tool to building skills and capabilities and acquiring access to opportunities and information. Build and save your database of contacts and continue to grow and expand the breadth of your network. Leverage your experiences and network of contacts to help others meet new people, gather information, or find a new job.

Stay connected to your industry.

Make sure you stay abreast of your changing industry. Stay involved in industry associations and professional organizations. Continue to build your knowledge of the industry through educational workshops, seminars, or trade journals. You have no guarantee that your company will stay independent or financially viable. You might be forced to look for a new job if your company merges, files for Chapter 11, or downsizes. You need to continue to build your knowledge and skills in your industry, thus continuing to increase your marketability.

Continue to build your personal effectiveness skills.

You are the only person who can manage your career. You need to make sure you are furthering your personal effectiveness skills. These skills refer to your formal education such as acquiring an MBA or professional certifications as well as enhancing your position competencies, business acumen, presentation skills, and leadership effectiveness skills.

Do not forget how to market yourself.

I recommend updating your résumé at least once a year. As your career grows, do not forget to capture your expanded job responsibilities, key accomplishments, successful projects, and significant results. Stay connected with the specific resources you successfully utilized to find your job, such as professional recruiting and staffing firms. Building a solid relationship with a recruiter you can trust can be a valuable asset as you grow in your career.

To further illustrate the suggestions about keeping yourself connected and marketable, let me share with you two stories of people who I have known in my career.

Susan joined a company that was growing and had a wonderful future. She worked hard, climbed the company ladder, and increased her earnings threefold. She was in the office early and stayed late. She earned a reputation in the company as a real winner and great contributor.

As the years progressed Susan continued to focus all her energy on her job. She worked too hard to meet new people outside of those who worked for the company. She dropped her membership in the industry associations and even discontinued her connections to her alumni association. Her network of people began to shrink, and her knowledge of everything except the narrow world of her company slowly slipped into the realm of historical data. In fact, I heard people refer to her as a "dinosaur." Everything about Susan was what she accomplished in the past, and nothing about her was current. In the same way that never using your muscles causes them to shrink and deteriorate, Susan's market value and personal network were withering.

After fifteen years with the company that Susan helped grow, the company was purchased by a competitor, which was great news for the owners but bad news for Susan. Her services were no longer needed, and she was out looking for a job. Her network was nonexistent. Her skills were outdated. In many ways, Susan was in no better shape for a job search than she was fifteen years before when she was a fresh graduate. It took her a year and a half to find a new job. She took a position that was lower in both salary and responsibility. If Susan continues to follow her narrow path of focus, she will most likely repeat her marginally successful career track.

In contrast, consider Mike's story. Mike, like Susan, was a young college graduate. He accepted a position with a large firm that had opportunities galore. Mike followed a much different path than Susan. He worked hard in the office but continued to keep a healthy focus on both growing his personal network and continuing to improve his personal effectiveness. Using the tuition reimbursement program offered by his firm, he enrolled in the local Executive MBA program, earning his MBA on his own time over three years of attending classes on Saturdays.

He remained active in the college alumni association in the city where he lived, accepting the position of president of that chapter. It took time to handle this position, but the contacts he made were immense. Mike was great at not only meeting and greeting people, but also taking the time to enter their names in his personal database. He was creative about keeping in touch with everyone he met. Whether it was a Christmas card or a phone call to ask a question of someone who might be more qualified, Mike stayed connected.

Mike seemed to squeeze so much into his week: lunch with someone from the Alumni Club, an evening meeting at his church to help with the new expansion plans, and golf with a group of business peers on Saturday. Mike was so well connected that I even called him at times to see if he could help me network to specific companies that I wanted to know better.

After six years in his first position, the company merged with a larger firm, and new management changed the culture. Mike was ready to move on. With the grace and speed of a deer, Mike put the word out through his network that he was interested in seeking a new opportunity. I can only imagine how people would describe Mike as they spread the word. "I know a guy who would be fantastic for any company that would be lucky enough to get him. He is smart, just earned his MBA, and is a very well-rounded professional." Within a few weeks Mike had the opportunity to meet with several companies that wanted him to join them. Exactly thirty-seven days after Mike decided to move on, he was sitting in his new office! Of course the first thing Mike did that night was e-mail his entire network letting them know of his new position, his new contact information, and how much he appreciated everybody's help.

Don't put this book in your attic, and don't put your career in jeopardy by ceasing your personal growth and networking. Keep this book on your bookshelf, ready to use again in three to five years. Keep your career healthy by building your personal network and continuing to learn.

May your achievements reach the stars and your successes light the night!

TIMOTHY J. AUGUSTINE

"Somehow I can't believe that there are any heights
that can't be scaled by a man who knows the secrets of
making dreams come true. This special secret, it seems to me,
can be summarized in four Cs. They are curiosity, confidence,
courage, and constancy, and the greatest of all is confidence.
When you believe in a thing, believe in it all the way,
implicitly and unquestionably."

Walt Disney

Index

About the Author

Timothy Augustine is a dynamic author and professional speaker who tours the nation presenting his How Hard Are You Knocking seminars to college students and professional organizations. Tim's unique background includes Human Resources and Strategic Marketing. As an Adjunct Professor at Illinois Institute of Technology's Stuart School of Business, Tim teaches Strategic Marketing in the MBA Program.

Tim is co-owner and managing partner of The Herman Draack Company, an international Human Resource Consulting Firm specializing in Executive Recruitment, Project Outsourcing and Human Resource Strategy Implementation with offices in Chicago, San Francisco and Washington D.C. An active member of Delta Sigma Pi Professional Business Fraternity, Society for Human Resource Management, and The Technical Recruiters Network of Chicago, Tim also serves on the Board of Directors for Open Heart Magic in Chicago. He is also a mentor for College Bound, a volunteer organization that provides scholarships, mentoring, and tutoring for Chicago-area high school students.

Tim's business career has been dedicated to developing and implementing human resource strategic programs. Examples include worldwide people strategies and Employer of Choice organizational initiatives. He has wide professional expertise in employee recruiting and selection, training and career development, benefit administration, salary and compensation programs, and in organizational communication and feedback processes.

A graduate of Northwestern University's Executive MBA Program, Tim also has degrees in Marketing and Speech Communications from Kent State University. He has served honorably in the United States Air Force National Guard.

Tim currently lives in the Chicago area with his wife and two children.

Contact Information:
www.howhardareyouknocking.com
Timaugustine@hermandraack.com